IOT 2030

IOT 2030

HOW THE WORLD IS BECOMING
MORE CONNECTED

CHONG HWAN KIM

NEW DEGREE PRESS

IOT 2030

How the World is Becoming more Connected

ISBN   978-1-64137-298-5   *Paperback*

          978-1-64137-483-5   *Ebook*

CONTENTS

PART 1

IOT AND WHY?

HOW TO READ
THIS BOOK

———

This book is about how new and existing technology can be used to improve our way of life. Even though it deals with a lot of what's happening in the business world, this book does not provide any hardcore financial data or any Old Testament theories of business schools. Yes, I am an MBA student, and like most of my peers, I love coming up with solutions to business-related problems and obsessing over incremental improvements for efficiency every day. However, I also believe that the future needs to be appreciated on a grander scale and also from a different perspective.

When speaking about the future, it is important to think critically and ask oneself, "Where is this all going?" "Who is going to benefit from it?" and "How will it impact our lives in the future?"

IoT (Internet of Things) is about finding a smart way of using the internet and sensor technology; I am sure readers would most likely assume from this that the two most important aspects of IoT (the internet and the sensor technology-infused wearable devices) is nothing new. I would like to emphasize that most of the technology being used in this book already exists; however, using this technology to collect a plethora of data and make determinable analysis for predicting user needs is the new innovation.

IoT is a method of creating a tangible benefit to one of the most valuable assets that is arising in the world: data. Throughout my study at Georgetown University, I have heard countless stories about how data is the most valuable asset (even more so than oil), and its value has been considered the next big gold mine for a lot of internet companies. But people are having a hard time seeing what data can do to improve people's lives.

Companies are trying to offer a tailored service for their individual customers beyond the internet and servers. For this to happen, there has to be data gathered about their customer's behavior. Sensor technology embedded in every existing wearable device and appliance will enable this to happen, and this is why IoT is the best solution to put data to use for the general population and not for the few internet companies that most people don't see every day. It's a way of democratizing the benefits of data.

So, in this book I will be talking about different aspects of how sensor technology can be implanted in our daily devices and be interconnected in ways to improve our lives and also attempt to make a summary of what this future will be like in a paragraph or two throughout the book. So if you are in a rush, just read the parts that say, "**So, how will this impact our future like the book says in 2030?**" and you will get the picture of what I am trying to say about using this technology. These sections will appear in different parts of the book as a way to quickly show you how all of this information and the developments involved with IoT can impact your life sooner than you think.

This book is divided into three parts. The first part is comprised of trying to define why I wrote this book, a brief definition of what IoT is, where it is going, and invisible benefits that are happening today in a general sense of things.

After the first part, I have divided the remainder into two sections. One section will be focused about our lives, our homes, and our families. It will delve deep into how this technology will improve our lives personally. The latter section

(Part 3) will be focused on how this technology will impact our working lives. IoT has a lot more applications at work than to our homes because you are talking about factories that are becoming self-aware about productivity with live connectivity and sensors all around its plant and logistics. So, it is logical for me to focus on the third part, making it the longest of all the parts.

Part 3 also deals with security concerns that come with having devices and the world becoming more connected; I am very aware that a connected world will also mean that our lives are more vulnerable for cyberterrorism activities. So yes, I want to talk to you about how important it is for us to be aware of the challenges we also face in terms of security issues that come with the world being more connected.

So now that I have explained what my book is about and how fun it is to understand the things that will make our lives less hectic, let's jump in and see the details and the stories I have prepared for you. Enjoy!

INTRO

WHY I CARE AND WHY YOU SHOULD TOO

———

Technology is always disrupting and improving people's lives. Just think about phones; for example, we moved from flip phones to smartphones within one generation, and in countries like South Korea, you can see almost everyone in the streets of Seoul (the nation's capital) using smartphones for transferring all sorts of data, whether it be talking to your friend on the phone or sending files to clients while on the run. It is fabulous to witness the fast changes in technology that is so dependent on the internet. Now we are looking at a future where multinational corporations or an international organization can exist on the internet and the physical need for an office will serve a different purpose to the working people in the twenty-first century.

This kind of technological advancement can impact everyone on all sorts of scales. Just imagine, your homework or your presentation materials will be available on your online drive where you can easily share it with the people you want at a click of a button. The days of whipping out your laptop and dragging the file in your hard drive as your attachment to your email is going to all be a bad experience you had in the past.

If your boss wants to fix your presentation material, he or she can go online and open the file in real time on the online cloud and make that minute change, and you don't have to save another revision file of your presentation because someone thought there should be a font change in your presentation. This is already possible in large multinational corporations like Samsung, where every file is shared and can be updated whenever an employee saves a file onto a shared file drive across all related employees. When I first joined Samsung in 2013, we still had to attach files to emails and save countless revision files on our hard drive if there needed to be a slight revision in our presentation files (or any data files) I couldn't leave the office until it was all done.

So, where does this all come in with IoT? Simply put, IoT is the sensor technology that brings the entire world together. Since companies are moving to have their entire operations done on the internet, it doesn't take much to figure out that: what companies and people are yearning for is better connectivity of data that is crossing devices and mediums of communications. This leads to the notion that there will be more demand for a better method of data collection as well. IoT will meet this growing demand and not only that it will enable companies to be more flexible in terms of finding data points that can help predict customer preferences better by enabling sensors to be embedded in all the incumbent devices, appliances, and equipment that are available in this world. This will lead to better ways to share data in real time so that consumers like you and I will be able to live life in a more productive and easy manner.

If companies are trying to be more flexible with the way they source raw materials or trying to vary prices faster to spur spending from their customers, they need better access to real-time data on what people want now so they can predict, support, or deliver the goods in an instant. This means you need to be more agile when communicating with your customers' needs. What better way is there to communicate if you can be allowed access to your customers' behavior? This is what IoT will bring.

Yes, there could be issues with security concerns because some might say that companies are going to be monitoring you 24/7, and I will be talking more about these concerns in Part 3. However, we have to look at the growing potential of the new economy that will run more efficiently and be more adaptable to trends and the needs of average Joes and Janes in the world. The world has already become more globalized with the internet, and it's about time we use it to make sure that our needs are met faster and more effectively.

So, why *is* technology moving so fast?

A CRASH COURSE ON IOT TECH

To understand where technology is coming from, we must understand the dynamics of its brain: starting with the chips (the semiconductors) that go into your devices. Semiconductor companies constantly innovate to make sure that new devices are being created to meet your daily demands.

If you think about it, progress is the nature of life and chips are always finding ways to be faster and better. Chip makers like Intel follow what's called Moore's law.

"Moore's law is the observation that the number of transistors in a dense integrated circuit doubles about every two years. The observation is named after Gordon Moore, *the cofounder of Fairchild Semiconductor and CEO of* Intel, *whose 1965 paper described a* doubling every year *in the number of components per integrated circuit, and projected this rate of growth would continue for at least another decade.*

In 1975, looking forward to the next decade, he revised the forecast to doubling every two years. The period is often quoted as eighteen months because of a prediction by Intel executive David House (being a combination of the effect of more transistors and the transistors being faster), and "Moore's prediction proved accurate for several decades and has been used in the semiconductor industry to guide long-term planning and to set targets for research and development."[1]

Semiconductors are the brains for all technology devices and servers that act as centers for transferring and saving data. Semiconductor companies like Nvidia, which supplies chips to IT companies like Amazon and Google[2], announced in March 2019 that it will acquire Mellanox Technologies Ltd., "an Israeli multinational supplier of computer networking products using InfiniBand and Ethernet technology."[3]

According to Jensen Huang, the CEO of Nvidia, "the acquisition will enable Nvidia to where everything is connected in the internet where our lives will be more diversely attached with one other through not just one device but through a

---

1   "Industrial Revolution." Wikipedia. Wikimedia Foundation, April 30, 2019.
2   Fitch, Asa. "Nvidia to Acquire Mellanox, Its Biggest Deal Ever at Roughly $7 Billion." The Wall Street Journal. Dow Jones & Company, March 11, 2019.
3   "Mellanox Technologies." Wikipedia. Wikimedia Foundation, October 5, 2019.

variety of products that were never digitized before."[4] The move toward complete digitalization of our economy requires great infrastructure and companies that are willing to invest in technology.

Now, I know you are wondering, what is this cloud computing and IoT? As a starter, cloud computing is defined in Wikipedia as "Cloud computing makes computer system resources, especially storage and computing power, available on demand without direct active management by the user. The term is generally used to describe data centers available to many users over the Internet."[5] This means that you can have organizations, companies, even governments, operating on the internet. Such powerful connectivity will open doors for real-time data sharing and decision-making. Imagine the dynamic change in business ecosystems that this will bring. I will be talking more about how this connectivity will be impacting our homes, our health, our cities, our businesses, and most importantly, our lifestyle in general.

When I first heard the term IoT, it was when I first joined Samsung in 2013. Back then, people were talking about wearable devices that would be as effective as a smartphone.

---

4   Fitch, Asa. "Nvidia to Acquire Mellanox, Its Biggest Deal Ever at Roughly $7 Billion." The Wall Street Journal. Dow Jones & Company, March 11, 2019.

5   "Cloud Computing." Wikipedia. Wikimedia Foundation, October 22, 2019.

Unfortunately, this has not happened, and it's not likely to be this way anytime soon. The IoT market will impact the market in a different way than what people had intended. It's a better way of measuring your lifestyle and augmenting one's productivity than being a device on its own that will bring innovation and a change to a way of life. Yes, I strongly believe that the next industrial revolution will be a way to boost (augment) our way of life to be more productive and innovative than to be a thing of its own that brings innovation.

HISTORY OF IOT

The "Internet of Things wave," a way to characterize what people in the IT industry were calling it five to ten years ago, was perceived as something phenomenal, but no one really knew what it was. That is because IoT is not just one device that will make a change, but it will be multiple devices that are incorporated with sensors, cameras, and robots (if necessary) to revamp the aspects of life that have been around since the first industrial revolution. I remember learning in history class in middle school that the invention of the steam engine changed the dynamics of how production is handled in the textile industry.

The term *industrial revolution*, if you look it up on Wikipedia, says it's "transition to new manufacturing processes in

Europe and the US, in the period from about 1760 to sometime between 1820 and 1840."[6] This is exactly what most people have misunderstood when it comes to what we call the industrial revolution. It's not so much on the focus of the end product, but it's about the changes in how we work, how we make stuff, and most importantly, how well we do our jobs with these augmentations in life. If you see below, the industrial revolution was about augmenting ways to get humans to produce better, which gradually leads to a better lifestyle.

This is a picture from Wikipedia of how the first industrial revolution changed the textile industry and how we were able

---

6   "Industrial Revolution." Wikipedia. Wikimedia Foundation,
     April 30, 2019.

to produce more textiles efficiently, which led to life-altering changes as a byproduct of this revolution.[7]

However, whenever I talk with my friends or acquaintances about the next industrial revolution, they think about how a single app changes the world, and we will be living in a world where machines are taking over instantaneously. What I think is the opposite: the innovation and the life-altering experience that people all assume will actually be a byproduct of a long line of incremental innovation that will happen in the next industrial revolution.

This innovation starts with sensors and I am going to be talking a lot about sensors, and these are the crux of what IoT is to the world that we live in. After talking with countless professionals that are working in this field, IoT is a device that incorporates sensors that can track movement, temperature, sound, and patterns in people's lives. The sensor technology is quite effective because it's been around in our lives for a while. When I was speaking with a professor at Georgetown, there was an example that when you get on an elevator, the elevator keeps its door open when it senses that people are entering and leaving. This technology has been around for a while (I mean, I remember having this technology being available since I was a child). Mass producing such sensors

---

7   "Industrial Revolution." Wikipedia. Wikimedia Foundation, April 30, 2019.

and incorporating them into our business environment to effectively gather data about our lives creates a new platform where our lives can be effectively lived with digitization.

This means that industrial adoption will most likely take place first, and then the effects from these innovations will spur into consumer benefits. These types of innovations will not likely be a story about a super-hot start-up that created a killer app or a new smart device that will revolutionize the world. This is a story about how large corporations (industrial or manufacturing) and governments work together to use this technology to revamp the economy and overall industrial efficiency to bring positive social impact for the public convenience to a new scale.

IOT INNOVATION EXAMPLES

One of the biggest examples that IoT is changing the world today is smart cities. Like what I said before, it is innovation that is taking place on a municipal scale and not something you will most likely hear from Silicon Valley. I will be talking more about smart cities in later chapters. I have spoken with people who worked on smart-cities projects and listened and spoken with high-ranking officials related to infrastructure and technology projects from think tanks in Washington, DC, and big companies (Fortune 500 types) that are leading technology in the field of infrastructure and smart cities.

One of the examples that I will briefly mention to entice your interest is about how these devices can impact energy conservation and cost savings in rural areas. I will be delving more deeply into this matter, but it is true that urbanization can come at a much cheaper cost than conventional methods of building infrastructure because the devices will enable projects to be viewed holistically by figuring out consumer demands more proficiently and in real time.

And this example has to do with farming. I did not really think about writing about farming when I was thinking of the Internet of Things. But there's so much water that's being wasted right now in farming. And if you can incorporate these drones and sets of devices that make up what IoT is, these sensors of Internet of Things get connected with networks benefiting all parts of life, starting with farmers and agriculture companies to cities and governments that lead to consumers and the general public to actively monitor water usage levels to conserve and save our precious resources.

There are places in this world that have drought issues during the summer, and some are very dependent on agriculture. And agriculture uses large amounts of water out of all the other sources of human activities. So, if there's going to be a foreseeable drought, we could use these technologies to make sure the water is used efficiently so that the cities will have enough water and supplies and energy and resources during unexpected droughts. Since agriculture takes a lot of water, with improvements in how farms use water by monitoring the water amounts flowing into our farms and controlling the usage more carefully, countries can use water in the best way for cities to get better access to new water supplies.

Speaking of cities, yes, this IoT technology can be incorporated in every dynamic of our infrastructure. Through incorporating multiple sensors into infrastructure projects, cities can go smart, meaning that cities will now be able to sense the inefficiencies of their surroundings and will make sure that they make changes to run in ways that can save costs and increase productivity. Public transportation, for example, when cities work on projects like making train subways and buses, routes are set separately, and project financing is done per contract for these public goods. However, with smart cities, these sensors all across the cities will have a better understanding of the city's current level of transportation volume and the lack of usage of existing routes and will incorporate such findings into the new blueprints of the entire transportation plans and have an artificial intelligence to structure the routes that will not be redundant with the existing infrastructure and create a cost-effective way of transporting the public.

This can make sure that the city can get the most efficient public transportation method by using these sensors and data to see where traffic is seeing congestion and see if any parts of the city need better water supplies during summertime. I have had discussions with people that are related in this field in Washington, DC, and the people that are involved in smart cities have said that the most and what can kind of routes will be experiencing the heaviest traffic and make sure that they could be public transportation caters to these contexts, conditions, and also the available capacity of transportation means.

I have worked in a company that makes electronic components. I have heard time and time again that automated manufacturing will be incorporated all around the world. And it will bring an industrial revolution that will impact all aspects of the manufacturing world, causing an increase in efficiency and save costs and make sure that innovation happens faster.

OKAY...BUT WHY IOT?

The example that I have provided above is the impact and the effects that such innovation will bring from an efficient revolution from industry, infrastructure, and innovation from the production side. I will be discussing these aspects more thoroughly over the book.

I believe IoT impact will be the biggest for the manufacturers, namely farmers. I wrote a little bit about farming and manufacturing and also wrote about cities as well. It's these old-school industries that will be revamped. IoT will bring efficient monitoring of these old methods of production and will create new opportunities to increase productivity. Increased productivity will bring new ways for these old industries to be faster and more agile, which can help conserve resources and build better infrastructure.

With that said, I believe this book is for people who want to know more about the unexpected benefits of IoT. I wrote this book to find out how technology will impact people's lives beyond a single device and the well-being of society holistically. If you are wondering about the untapped possibilities of IoT or the future of technology, that's what this book is all about. Or, if you're clueless about what IoT stands for, I think this book will help lend a perspective toward what you are trying to understand about the next wave of innovation.

When my parents first bought their cellphones, I remember talking to them about the unfathomable opportunities that it would bring and the prevalent potential it has in the future. It always takes a lot of effort to teach something new, especially technology, and people are used to what they were using in the past. I am not saying my parents are slow learners (they are far smarter than I am), but we all have had learning curves for smartphones. My book is designed for people to understand the various applications to make the learning experience a lot easier for the human mind.

SO, HOW WILL THIS START?

If you read the tech section of any newspaper, there is always a mention about the latest trends in network connectivity. For example, if you go to the tech section of *The Wall Street Journal*, there is most likely to be at least one article a day that will talk about 5G, autonomous driving, semiconductors, machine learning, or IoT. According to Wikipedia,

"5G (from 5th Generation) is the latest generation of cellular mobile communications. It succeeds the 4G(LTE-A, WiMax), 3G (UMTS, LTE) and 2G (GSM) systems. 5G performance targets high data rate, reduced latency, energy saving, cost reduction, higher system capacity, and massive device connectivity."[8]

Every generation connectivity had its advantages; for example, 3G connectivity-built ways for data transfers that enabled devices like iPhones to become prevalent in our daily lives.

My boss used to tell us that component tech requirements became a lot more stricter with the advent of the smartphones because, simply put, you need more computing power in your phone if you want to watch your YouTube video and text your friends at the same time with your handheld device. Like I said earlier, IoT is set to take the stage on a scale that will encompass our daily lives through massive amounts

---

8   "5G." Wikipedia. Wikimedia Foundation, October 25, 2019

of data connectivity. Through my time at Georgetown University, I have attended many sessions in think tanks like Brookings Institute and CSIS (Center for Strategic and International Studies) that discussed the changes that 5G will bring. I strongly believe that 5G will give enough connectivity power to connect the world, but we must understand how this will change our lives. This chapter will delve deep into the possible effects that this will have.

In an effort to explain how great 5G is compared to our existing 4G, I am referencing information that I have seen on Verizon's (one of the largest wireless carriers in the US) website to illustrate its benefits.

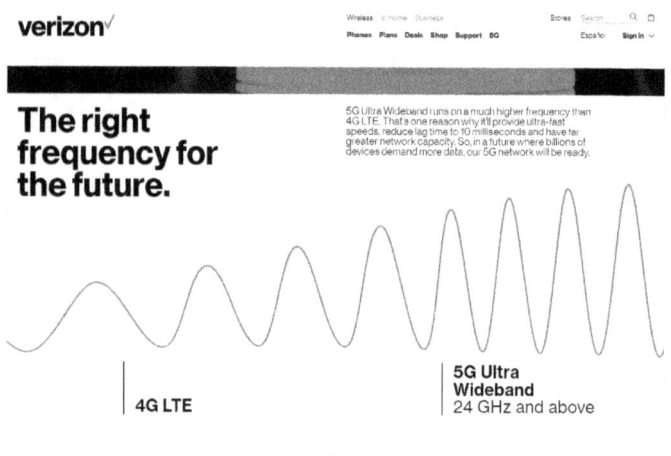

9

---

9   "Verizon 5G: This Is 5G Built Right." Verizon. Accessed October 27, 2019.

The picture above explains how 5G will give better speed for connectivity. To put it in business terms, the 5G ultrawide band will provide greater network capacity. Increased capacity will give businesses more leeway to be more agile and flexibility to carry and transfer information at a greater speed. This will make all sorts of information travel faster on multiple fronts, making a platform for billions of IoT devices to be available to send and receive information about user preference and enhanced productivity. Having sensors connect to each other to gather immense amount of data and deciphering this data through AI (artificial intelligence) to create recommendations and best course of action will save time, energy, and resources that are all finite to us.

If you want your car to drive itself, it will need more than just cameras to determine how close you are to the car in front of you and what degree of turns that is necessary to park itself. It needs sensors to tell where and how fast the traffic is for better prediction. Also, the advanced connectivity for the sensor data to be shared so that any accidents can be averted if there is a foreseeable problem in distances ahead.

With that said, the development and deployment of 5G and IoT must move together. Such intricate connectivity can create a world where data flowing from sensors in people's wearable devices to devices for traffic sensors to monitor traffic speed can happen instantly... Tremendous amounts of data will transfer all across the dynamics of life, and this demands faster connectivity on a larger scale. Therefore, there needs to be a clear understanding about IoT and 5G. Two different aspects need to be considered where 5G only concentrates on the speed of the transmit and IoT wearable devices are about the contents, the wearable market is highly dependent on providing connectivity within devices so that users can have more real experiences using these devices, this has to do more with the contents provided then the connectivity speed itself.

I was interviewing Dong Yon Kim, who is the South Korean author of the book *Unintended Future*. He said that the technology that will be proliferating from the deployment of sensor technology and 5G network will enable autonomous driving vehicles. There has been news on the internet that such a development was put into action, and if you visit Tesla's website, it talks more about how autonomous vehicles have saved lives.

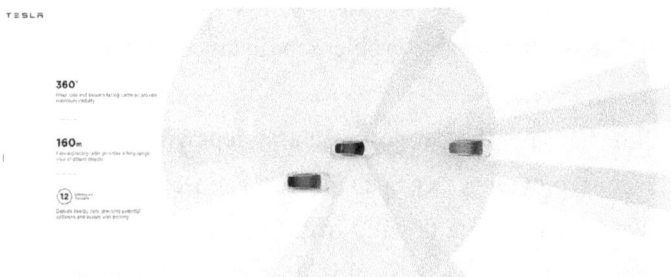

The picture above can be viewed from Tesla's website on its model S and how its sensors are used for lane keep assist and collision avoidance.[10]

Also, when talking about the benefits of 5G, telecommunications company KT made commercials on the benefits of 5G using IoT that are available on YouTube and explain higher connectivity from 5G in better context.

Pictured above is a depiction of what the future will be like if KT's 5G and shipbuilders like Hyundai work to make IoT incorporated in their daily operations. The video can be accessed via YouTube in the following URL: https://www.youtube.com/watch?v=oM1kloI3s4k.

---

10   https://www.tesla.com/models

If you have seen the video, it tells you how the technology will be impacting the way shipbuilding companies can conduct inspections on their ships by looking at components, which are manufactured with sensors implanted in them that diagnose any issues through the smart glasses of an inspector and make sure any potential problems can be avoided before the ship is set for sail. This technology can immensely decrease the risks of any catastrophes at sea. Also, cameras and sensors that are attached in manufacturing plants will be able to monitor the progress of each manufacturing phase in real time to make sure that all safety regulations are met and to control production speed and raw material procurement. All details about the benefits of IoT and manufacturing will be dealt with in subsequent chapters, but this chapter is to emphasize the enormous potential IoT can have with 5G. Also, other than companies, I will be providing more examples on how enhanced connectivity through 5G can unlock the potential of 5G to bring true digital transformation.

SO, HOW WILL THIS IMPACT OUR FUTURE LIKE THE BOOKS SAYS IN 2030?

Fascinating stuff is happening with technology. Out of curiosity, I briefly asked five of my MBA classmates what to expect when asked about the next big thing that is going to happen in innovation. All five of them were expecting a blockbuster device or something very, very new that no one has never heard of in the history of mankind. But the truth cannot be further than their beliefs. I was fortunate enough to take Professor Eric Koester's Innovation and Intrepreneurship class over the summer of 2019 at Georgetown University McDonough School of Business. It's a fascinating class that challenges the way we think about how we can influence innovation in organizations and create something new. And what Professor Koester said about innovation was that 77 percent of innovation takes place in incumbent product improvement. IoT belongs in this category: it's using the tools we have today and upgrading them so your tools connect with each other to know your patterns so that your life will be tailored for improvement and better productivity. This book talks about a future where the old has been revamped, which will provide a foundation for breakthrough products like the iPhone. This book sees the future where the methods of yielding crops will be changed so that every civilization on earth can enjoy nutritious food and clean water, a future where work–life balance was a concern of the past, and most importantly, a future where we can provide a stepping-stone for growth and blockbuster products to come in the future.

THE RETURN OF THE "HAS BEENS"

Smart city and smart infrastructure: making farming hot again!

One of the prime examples that is being used for smart cities is how water irrigation systems are being used to better manage the water usage for this finite natural resource that most people like me used to take for granted: Water. As George Hawkins, the former CEO of District of Columbia Water and Sewer Authority said in a conference at a 2016 sustainability forum, water utility is essential for survival and converting water to energy and the reliability of that should be a paramount factor.[11]

I was taking one of the intensive classes at Georgetown McDonough School of Business called Business of Water with professor Mark Giordano. In this class, Professor Giordano addressed the finite matter of water in ways that only a very small fraction of this resource is usable for our daily lives (for example, drinking and agricultural usage) and that there needs to be a better way of managing our water and there are underlying ways of using technology to make farming costs effective and cities be more aware of the water usage to make sure that rural areas will have more resources during drought seasons.

Below, an article in *The Economist* talks about the scarcity of water; when I asked my classmates at Georgetown, they

---

11 Lcrenshaw. "2016 Sustainability Forum." U.S. Chamber of Commerce Foundation, October 24, 2019

too were amazed by how little we knew about the limits of this resources.[12]

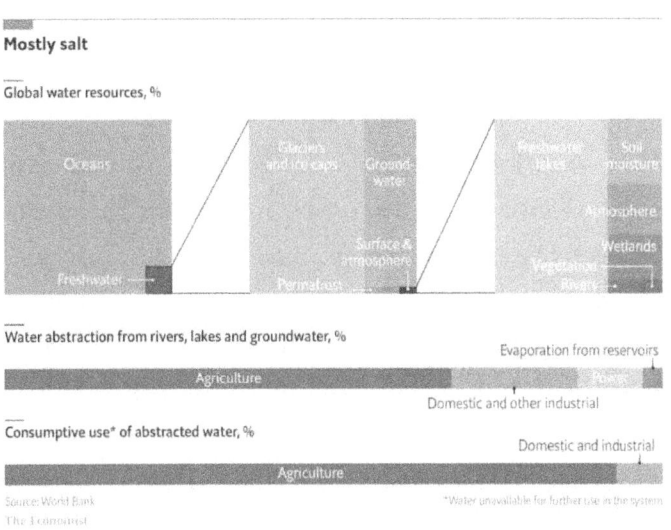

Mostly salt

Global water resources, %

Water abstraction from rivers, lakes and groundwater, %

Evaporation from reservoirs

Agriculture | Power

Domestic and other industrial

Consumptive use° of abstracted water, %

Domestic and industrial

Agriculture

Source: World Bank
The Economist

°Water unavailable for further use in the system

Definition for the drawing above: Abstracted water is derived from "Water abstraction," which "refers to the process of taking or extracting water from a natural source (rivers, lakes, groundwater aquifers, etc.) for various uses, from drinking to irrigation, treatment, and industrial applications."[13]

---

12   "Climate Change and Population Growth Are Making the World's Water Woes More Urgent." The Economist. The Economist Newspaper, February 28, 2019.

13   Cooper, and Brent Cooper. "The Abstraction of Water." Medium. The Abs-Tract Organization, February 18, 2018.

"The fundamental problems, however, are neither the resource itself, since water is likely to remain abundant enough even for a more populous Earth, nor technical. They are managerial, or, more precisely, how to withstand economic, cultural, and political pressures to mismanage water."[14]

Also, when I was speaking with Professor Giordano, he emphasized that IoT can be used in multiple ways to increase productivity on farms. In an email conversation, he mentioned that agriculture does use most of the water and getting access for water is the most important aspect of farming. However, institutional mechanisms that will allow farmers to save water must also be implemented. This is where IoT comes in: cities must find ways to invest in technology that can provide the necessary infrastructure that could promise a steady stream of safe and efficient water supplies. The increase in margin and revenue opportunity from farming will enable increases in governments to retrieve the amount invested in the farming infrastructure from the increased opportunities that farming will bring to its local community and also related businesses that the government can collect more taxes from.

---

14 "Climate Change and Population Growth Are Making the World's Water Woes More Urgent." The Economist. The Economist Newspaper, February 28, 2019.

However, there are core technologies that are being implemented for agricultural and municipal use to distribute water effectively and save costs. There was an opinion article in *The New York Times*, "Water Is Broken. Data Can Fix It" by Charles Fishman. This article opens up the possibility of using data to proficiently manage the water usage in agriculture that can manage their input levels and can maximize the output (much like how manufactures do with their operations).[15]

Just imagine the advantage that a farmer can have in harvesting if their equipment is infused with sensors (IoT devices) that can gather information on moister levels of the soil as they gather their crops. The sensors will automatically register the moist level of the soil and beam the data, through a satellite system, to the farming company on the level of yield that can be projected for future crops. Therefore, farms can forecast the level of water that will be needed to maintain the output. The data will be shared with nearby cities so that it can be used as a measure to predict droughts and water demand for the upcoming season. If the cities and local officials are better aware of the water levels needed by the agricultural industries, they can advise the public to be more cautious on their water usage so that the cities can

---

15   Fishman, Charles. "Water Is Broken. Data Can Fix It." The New York Times. The New York Times, March 17, 2016.

divert more attention to helping out farms that can have a negative impact from the expected drought.

This could have a tremendous positive effect on how we can save water and not waste one of most essential natural resources to our lives. According to savethewater.org, the increasing usage of water is causing disconcerting facts. For example, the world population is likely to face severe or chronic water shortages by 2025, while there is an anticipated 40 percent increase in demand for fresh water by 2030.[16]

George Hawkins also mentioned that the water and sewage infrastructure needs to be updated where median age of water pipes are seventy-nine years old. Mr. Hawkins mentioned that some pipes in DC were installed before the Civil War; now that is some old infrastructure, and any equipment or machine that old I assume will be very inefficient. Therefore, you could also imagine the kind of inefficiencies in handling our natural resources. If cities and industries make sure that they can incorporate IoT into their businesses by effectively managing water usage through sensors on sprinklers and water pipes, then we can make sure that cities and farms do not suffer from water shortages in case of droughts. For a better understanding of effective water usage via IoT, there is

---

16   "Water Facts." Save The Water™. Accessed May 19, 2019.

a website, wateruseitwisely.com, that explains the possibility of how IoT devices can be used to conserve water.

SPRINKLER SYSTEMS

- Sprinklers can cover large areas.
- Manual sprinklers require you to open the valve, time the watering yourself and then shut off the flow.
- Automatic sprinkler systems offer the benefit of programmable controllers.
- Make sure you set automatic sprinklers correctly and adjust it as conditions change.
- Water early in the morning to reduce the evaporation rate.
- If water runs off your yard, split your watering times into two or more sessions.
- Be sure to turn off your system if you're getting enough water from rain showers.

DRIP IRRIGATION

- This system is good for a small yard or for watering individual plants.
- Drip irrigation is highly effective at supplying one to four gallons of water per hour directly to the soil.
- The advantage of drip irrigation over sprinklers is that there is little water loss due to evaporation or runoff.
- It's particularly good for mulched areas because it can directly soak the soil without washing away the mulch.

HAND WATERING

- The simplest and most common irrigation system is a garden hose or a portable sprinkler.
- The advantage of hand watering is that you can easily avoid over watering.
- Use a nozzle to control the flow.
- When water stops being absorbed into the ground, move to another location.
- Wait an hour, and then plunge a long screwdriver or space into the ground to check that the soil is moist to a depth of six to ten inches.

Picture above was taken from wateruseitwisely.com[17]

Cities can also adapt these sensors to forecast weather patterns and make sure that traffic is controlled in a manner so that people will control CO_2 emissions and control public transportation. In an interview with Chris Magnan, a project manager at GDIT (General Dynamics Information Technology, Inc.) who leads a team of experts on smart city projects, he talked about projects where cities are incorporating the latest network (5G) and sensor technology all across cities to manage traffic control. Magnan mentioned that "the

---

17 "Efficient Irrigation | Water Saving Irrigation Methods." Water Use It Wisely. Accessed May 19, 2019.

city of London uses sensors and policy to decrease traffic density [London has cameras to impose a £12 charge during the weekdays; this policy reduced traffic density]." Hence, imagine the city can control the traffic congestion by utilizing past data and the current streams of data gathered from countless cameras and sensors in the city to make every car in the streets have navigation to direct the car onto other routes prior to any congestion. This will enable savings on a massive scale from emissions to time that people will have spent on roads.

Magnan also mentioned that smart cities projects can reduce income gaps between the rich and poor and that "the World Bank has identified smart city as a gateway out of poverty [service automation and cost reduction which ideally reduces economic barriers]." If you go to the World Bank's website, it has a very interesting article about how smart cities will increase sustainability and cost reduction that will make development more affordable for countries.

THE $2.57 TRILLION MARKET: THE NEW FRONTIER FOR GROWTH

IoT in city infrastructure will also not only making the cities be more affordable but also decrease unnecessary costs related to infrastructure projects. If you travel to one of the older cities in this world and take public transportation, there will be a time when you get on the bus and you are the only person in it. You begin to wonder why this bus operates at this time and route when there is a subway right underneath its route. The bus is not only wasting public resources but also is polluting by emitting CO_2 into the environment. If we have capable sensors and data analytics in place for smart cities, municipalities will be able to effectively reduce the unnecessary costs but also be more efficient in saving the environment.

"Many of today's largest metropolises are an organizational and infrastructural nightmare. Take the city of Atlanta, for example. The greater metropolitan area of Atlanta supports a population of about 2.5 million people and spans 137 kilometers between its two furthest points. By 1990, this sprawl had established a density of six people per hectare. Now, compare Atlanta to a city with a similar level of population, Barcelona. The furthest distance of built up area in Barcelona is 97 kilometers with a density of 176 people per hectare.[18] *The contrast between the densities of Atlanta and Barcelona can be observed in the diagram left from Alain Bertaud, 2002. The respective densities of Atlanta and Barcelona greatly affect the cities' ability to serve their citizens. For example, in order for Atlanta to accommodate as many people as Barcelona's public transit system, Atlanta would need to build an additional*

18   "World Development Report 2009." WDRs - World Development Report 2009. Accessed May 19, 2019.

3,400 kilometers of track and about 2,800 new metro stations. Atlanta could then support 30 percent of trips through mass transit which Barcelona accomplishes with only 99 kilometers of tracks and 136 stations."[19]

This paragraphs explains how smart cities can make public transportation and infrastructure at a much cheaper cost due to the interconnectivity of the different transportation methods in the cities to effectively target the places for development that will create the maximum benefits for municipals to serve their population. Magnan also mentioned that smart cities is predicted to be a $2.57 trillion (yes, trillion) market by 2025, based on Barcelona's drastic improvements using such efficient methods of smart cities by utilizing smart devices and connectivity to bring maximum efficiency to its people at a fraction of the cost of cities in much richer countries. This investment will surely being a net impact that can reduce poverty.

High-paying jobs, from the need of automation and the cost reduction for small businesses to enter the field, will be a way to reduce the income gap from this new project. For example, developing countries will be able to modernize their cities at a cheaper cost that can foster an infrastructure for the nation to grow effectively.

---

19   "What Is a Smart City and How Can a City Boost Its IQ?" World
      Bank Blogs. Accessed May 19, 2019

According to an article from information-age.com, when cities adopt smart city technology by using IoT to urbanize their rural areas, the cost savings by using such technology will be immense. The article made its statement based on a paper by ABI Research. ABI Research provides strategic guidance for visionaries needing market foresight on the most compelling transformative technologies"[20], and the cost savings projected from this research institute estimated that smart cities could lead to cost savings of $5 trillion by 2022. Smart cities consist of "automation, artificial intelligence, along with sensors, data-sharing, and analytics will all be critical in helping cities save costs."[21]

Here are some of the key cost saving amounts that municipals can achieve by adapting this technology, according to information-age.com:

"Key cost savings from the ABI Research report highlight that, in each such typical smart mega city of the future:

- Governments: Could save as much as $4.95 billion annually. Street lighting and smart buildings are two areas that could yield savings, with smart street lights expected to cut repair and maintenance costs by 30 percent.

20 "About US." ABI Research: for visionaries. Accessed May 19, 2019.
21 "Smart Cities Could Lead to Cost Savings of $5 Trillion." Information Age,

- Enterprises: A $14 billion cost-saving opportunity exists for enterprises, in areas that include freight transportation by using more energy efficient transport options, such as drones, robots or driverless vans and trucks, and smart manufacturing plants.
- Citizens: Savings up to $26.69 billion per year could be achieved in areas such as utilities, through the deployment of smart meters and micro-grid, and in education with the deployment of a hybrid education system (physical and online)."[22]

The primary motivation for smart cities is to automate services and reduce the cost of services.

More examples can be found on the smart cities counsel website. The smart cities council informs on the latest developments on smart city projects, and there has been success in small scale projects like airports that enhance productivity and save costs in areas that had been operating in an old-fashioned manner. For example, an example, the website mentions how San Diego International Airport has successfully incorporated IoT into their operations:

"San Diego International Airport is already on the smart parking path. Its newest garage has a state-of-the-art parking

22 "Smart Cities Could Lead to Cost Savings of $5 Trillion." Information Age, May 15, 2018.

guidance system that directs customers quickly to the nearest open space. (The garage is also sustainable, with extensive natural lighting, energy-efficient fixtures, and a stormwater re-use system that captures and treats rainwater for use in the airport's Central Utility Plant.)"[23]

If such technology can be incorporated on a massive scale, say like in New York City, the level of cost-saving opportunities and solutions for better municipal management can be offered where populations will be able to make better use of finite resources while creating more opportunities for affluence in the future.

5G, THE NEW PLATFORM, DO WE NEED CONTENT OR PLATFORM FIRST?

5G is the future; there are loads of conversations going back and forth in many think tanks in Washington, DC, about what this is and how it will benefit our lives. 5G and IoT will most likely impact the business to business environment more than consumer businesses since the ways businesses are doing their B2B (Business to Business) transactions have not improved when 4G-led innovation allowed people to make payments through their phones at any shops you

---

23 "Discover the Smart Airport That's Teaching Lessons to Smart Cities (and See It in Action)." Smart Cities Council Accessed May 19, 2019.

go to in the world. Projects like smart cities and automated manufacturing are many times bigger than the smart home and consumer wearable market since they have not been revamped for so long (remember the $2.57 trillion dollar market size for smart cities).

There will be more opportunities for companies to utilize the new platform to enhance their presence on the web. Companies will be able to effectively transport their goods and services to each player in the supply chain, from manufacturers to wholesale distributors. This can also mean that 5G will create opportunities for new content to be created in sectors that were not used to having technology for their strategic advantage. This means enabling hospitals and raw material manufacturers and farmers adopting new technology to cut costs and offer better solutions to their customers that will enable a proliferation of profitable opportunities. Much like what each generation of connectivity has done for the people that have used it in the past, 5G will have as much of a positive effect as it did with their predecessors. For that I will have to explain more about the past impacts that connectivity leaps have caused around the world.

Technological quantum leap is something we all hope will happen that will magically improve our lives. It has always come in different ways. Thanks to my parents, I have had wonderful experiences growing up in places like Washington,

DC, Seoul, Geneva, Jakarta, and New Delhi; all of them places of great innovation that is fostered from a close cooperation between private and public sectors. Every day you see friends whose parents have been involved in technology or tech related policymaking. Whenever I see countries becoming more relevant in technology advancement, I always have the urge to know: Does innovation happen when the infrastructure necessary to foster technology happens first, or does the private sector create the content for it that spurs public financing of such projects to follow?

When the world first met 3G, it was a quantum leap from what we had at 2G connectivity. 3G connectivity provided such a boost in connectivity that people were able to watch their favorite TV shows on YouTube and share pictures and locations with their friends and loved ones. I remember when the first iPhone was released in July 2007. I heard colleagues who were in the IT industry during that time, and they too remember the day that the first iPhone came to the market and changed the way people will share and send information forever.

I was in college at that time, and I couldn't afford the iPhone when it was first released; yes, iPhones were expensive then as are they now, and I was very content with just sending messages and calling people through my 2G flip phone. I didn't know how outdated my phone was until I saw my roommate's new iPhone. But what struck me then and what still strikes me now is this paradigm shift in people's lives from technology. It was indeed a technology miracle. It was like seeing the internet for the very first time; when it first appears, it looks like an enigma, but when content is created, and people to try it out for themselves, then it becomes crystal clear that it will benefit and make things more convenient.

Making sure the general public has access to the new connectivity speed is an infrastructure project, so it works a lot like a highway. Let's imagine in a world where people are riding horses (my most comparative analogy to a 2G flip phone in 2007), and the country decided to pursue a major infrastructure project and build highways for goods to travel safely and in large quantities, faster, all at once, to boost trade and development within the urban and rural areas (the highway will be 3G and boosting trade and development is to make information travel faster than before). Such a project was never seen in this country because trade was just a mere barter between merchants who rode their horses, which could withstand any terrain. Since these transactions happened on a one to one or small group basis, the quantity and the frequency was little to none for some rural areas. Hence, rural areas had no access to the plentiful resources that the people who lived in urban cities were enjoying.

But now with the highway, all urban areas and rural areas are connected via a large asphalt-based road. Horses can certainly run better, and there can be more trade. And let's say that one innovative company launches a new machine called an automobile (yes, the automobiles here are my best comparison to the iPhones). Now the automobiles can fully utilize the highways and travel a lot faster and carry more quantity at once and more frequently to any destination that a merchant pleases (assuming gasoline prices are equal to feeding horses). This will enable more trade and creation of wealth on a scale that has never seen before. This is possible because of infrastructure projects that made it possible for private sectors to be innovative and take advantage of the new platform that has been provided. 3G worked the same way. First it was provided to the people, then businesses started releasing flip phones with internet connectivity, then Apple came and changed the way we see and hear and learn things. Most innovation, whether it's technology or manufacturing, infrastructure must be there first. A playground must be there first in order for kids to create the coolest catch game.

Take manufacturing, for example. According to the National Science and Technology Council, the factors that impact innovation and competitiveness for advanced manufacturing are "The growth of advanced manufacturing requires advances in technology-based infrastructure. Technological innovation is closely tied to manufacturing capability. Global leadership in innovation is required for American manufacturers to maintain (and in some cases regain) their competitive edge. While rapid innovation has long been a defining attribute of American industry, private investments in manufacturing-based technologies have dramatically shrunk in recent years as investors focused on the rapid return on investments possible through software-based start-ups. Public investment in basic and early-stage applied research, along with public-private R&D partnerships, can help drive private sector investment and innovation in advanced. Hence manufacturing will be the bedrock for new growth in our economy and we should all be aware of what it could bring to our future."[24]

SO, HOW WILL THIS IMPACT OUR FUTURE LIKE THE BOOK SAYS IN 2030?

There is an old Greek proverb: "A society grows great when old men plant trees whose shade they know they shall never sit in."[25] I am a strong believer in this proverb and believe that a road has to be paved first for the next generation to

24 "Strategy for American Leadership in Advanced Manufacturing." Strategy for American Leadership in Advanced Manufacturing. SUBCOMMITTEE ON ADVANCED MANUFACTURING COMMITTEE ON TECHNOLOGY, October 2018.

25 "Greek Proverb Quote 'A Society Grows Great When Old Men Plant Trees Whose Shade They Know They Shall Never Sit in." Wisdom Home Decor Print Wall Art." Amazon. Amazon. Accessed May 19, 2019.

enjoy the benefits and create means to make society thrive from that setting provided by their forefathers in our modern world. I believe that IoT can truly bring the interconnectivity and the convenience to the people in the future.

Currently, such movement is taking place by people who are working in government and in the private sector. Marjorie Dickman and John Godfrey, co-chair, National IoT Strategy Dialogue, who are working at Intel and Samsung Electronics America, published a report with Vince Jesaitis, vice president, Government Affairs at Information Technology Industry Council, that stated,

"Strategic recommendations for the US government to work with industry to drive American IoT leadership. We are eager to support Congress and the Trump Administration in taking these steps to create a policy and regulatory environment that will attract unparalleled private sector investment and innovation in the IoT, thereby modernizing the nation's infrastructure, improving American manufacturing, and growing GDP. We thank all of the individuals, organizations, and government entities that collaborated with us throughout this process and look forward to collaboratively advancing these strategic recommendations and achieving US IoT leadership."

The report also estimates that "IoT will produce a total economic impact of \$3.9 to \$11 trillion per year globally by

2025, equivalent to 11 percent of the world economy." Hence, there is some wisdom in the word that innovation comes when government provides the playground for innovation to happen.[26]

However, we cannot just count on the government to create a platform just to see innovation. I do not know if we need the platform first or the content. But I can say that all generations of connectivity were able to bring growth and opportunity that brought the next evolutions of business and industry through a synergy of both the public and private sectors.

So, whenever you are watching your favorite channel on You-Tube or Netflix, please be reminded that there are people that worked hard to set up the necessary infrastructure for the wireless internet connectivity and the smartphones for enabling your favorite content to be created and shared easily.

Hence, the future I am talking about is this: whatever you have been witnessing for the past ten years—the connectivity through your phone and your laptop is the most distinguishing one—think of this happening with all of your appliances when IoT hits mainstream. And this will only be possible because businesses and governments today are working

---

26   Garfeld, Dean C, Marjorie Dickman, John Godfrey, and Vince Jesaits. "National IOT Strategy Dialogue." National IOT Strategy Dialogue, 2016.

on connecting the world faster and implementing devices to make them communicate with each other safely so that future generations can reap the benefits of living productive and happy lives.

PART 2

AT HOME

So the story starts…

Jane and Bob Kim are a married couple living in Seoul. Jane is a working mom working in one of the prominent conglomerates in Korea. Jane and Bob have two children and work-life balance is clearly a struggle for double income couples. However, thanks to the digital transformation, Jane and Bob are not too worried about balancing work and doing housework.

When Jane leaves for work, she gets into her car and asks her built-in navigation to look for grocery shops near her apartment that offer the best quality ingredients for making lasagna for four people. Her navigation quickly connects with the smart refrigerator at home and assesses the level of freshness of the existing ingredients. After analysis, the navigation gives a brief report on the kind of ingredients are in her smart refrigerator and sorts out the ingredients needed to cook lasagna for her family.

Jane's navigation uses the data received from the smart refrigerator to recommend nearby supermarkets that sell these ingredients. Jane looks through the grocery stores that sell the ingredients and sorts them by the best quality offered via customer satisfaction data gathered from the internet. Jane chooses the mart she wants to go to. The navigation directs her to the nearest route by checking the current traffic conditions. The current traffic conditions and the average speed of cars on the roads are visible thanks to the smart city project that enabled sensors to track traffic in real time.

She can also have the option of having the car drive itself if she is too tired at an extra cost since it will utilize more data than driving it herself. Also, the navigation alerts her if there is a car coming from an intersection at a higher-than-average speed and slows down her speed if her car is going faster than the average driver in Seoul.

When Jane reaches her grocery store, the data in her navigation gets transferred to her smartphone, where she can use it to find her way around the store to get the ingredients. Also, the smartphone searches and organizes data that is gathered from the sensors available in the mart to tell her which ingredients have better deals so that Jane can calculate the next best alternative if she wants to switch out an ingredient.

When she is done picking her groceries, she can immediately take the groceries to the car without having to go through the checkout counter because every product has an RFID chip embedded in the packaging that recognizes the purchases. RFID is an acronym for "radio-frequency identification" and refers to a technology whereby digital data encoded in RFID tags or smart labels are captured by a reader via radio waves.[27]

Also, since the checkout counters are also embedded with sensors that are in configuration with the mart's AI, the automated checkout counter can determine what Jane has purchased in the past and compare it with what she bought today to offer greater deals on items she could buy in the future to incentivize her to come back for more shopping in the future.

For payment, Jane authorizes the payment via her smartphone, and the groceries are purchased; this could be bad for companies that are making wallets, but with IoT technology, wallets are a thing of the past.

27 "What Is RFID and How Does RFID Work? - AB&R®." AB&R, September 11, 1970.

When Jane gets in her car and drives to her home, the sensors in her car will automatically learn that she is leaving the grocery store and is heading back home. The fact that she is on the move will be noticed via the sensors embedded in her car, and such information will be transferred from her navigator to her AI butler at home, which will then coordinate her arrival settings via her smart home devices.

At her home, the smart LED lights will light up before her estimated time of arrival, the smart oven will start to preheat to match her estimated time of arrival, the smart air controller unit will make sure that the air is fresh and the temperature is just right for cooking (per Jane's preference) via central heat/cooling/air filter technology.

By the time she arrives at her front door, the sensor will acknowledge her retinal scan and the door will be unlocked automatically. Jane will be ready to cook her dinner and serve her family the delicious lasagna that she had planned since she got off work.

Smart kitchen technology has already prepped the oven for her. The smart kitchen will also receive data of what she did after she left work and will recommend the recipe to create lasagna that is suited for her family. The smart kitchen also has data of how seasoning is used for each meal, so it can recommend on how much salt they usually eat or how spicy they need the lasagna to be. Also, if there is a family member with health problems, the smart kitchen will also advise against using more salt. With the help of her smart devices, Jane is able to finish cooking the lasagna before her family arrives without any hassle.[28]

So…What Does This All Mean?

The above story is an example of what life will be like in the future if the IoT business (a sensor-based analytics system) actually becomes a part of our lives. I am going to talk about the potential of the IoT industry to illustrate why it's a gold mine. I have heard countless stories from IT professionals that data is the most valuable asset. I would like to add to this by saying that IoT is where this value translates to mankind. From my point of view, this is the next great battlefield for the tech firms of the world, and companies in all aspects of the technology ecosystem should be gearing up for the next industrial revolution that is the world of digital transformation.

Let's continue the story of Jane Kim and her life as a working mom in the future of 2030. Let's assume that she lives in a world where 5G is fully connected and with its full potential with smart cities infrastructure realized. She is in a place

---

28 "Refrigerator." Wikipedia. Wikimedia Foundation, May 5, 2019.

where every city in the world is well suited for sensors to be prevalent in our lives. This makes her life in a setting where massive data collection and analytics is not a new thing but a reality where it can create tangible value. Now, let's see how her life can be better than the normal Jane's of today.

Jane's life will be more convenient because her life pattern can be analyzed more thoroughly to make sure she can get the most out of her time in any given activities that she will be engaged in. So, when Jane gets back home from work, she cannot only use the smart refrigerator to make sure that her life is synced with other members of the family (like what I have written in the intro) but also her smart home will have an artificial intelligence that acts as a central controller of all the data gathered about Jane and her family and will able to predict and pursue actions that can satisfy Jane's next moves.

This description may remind you of a very popular figure in current pop culture. Yes, it's Jarvis, Tony Stark's trusty AI butler from the Marvel Cinematic Universe's *Iron Man* movies! In that movie, the AI gathers data from every sensor applied in his household.

Remember the first *Iron Man* movie? Tony Stark frequently talks to Jarvis, who controls every aspect of what's going on in the household and acts like a human butler to meet Tony Stark's needs. Well, that movie nailed what smart homes are supposed to do for our lives in the future. The following part will talk more about how these sensor technologies that are implanted in home appliances can gather data about the user and also have a system in place to analyze the person's behavior and predict the user's next move to recommend sets of options to make their lives much easier and more productive.

I mean, just think about it: imagine when you walk into your apartment and your household, AI has already turned on the lights and controlled the room temperature, made the self-activating vacuum cleaner clean the house, and also has the oven pre-heated so that you can eat your favorite meal when you go home instead of walking into a cold, empty, dark, messy house just to have a decent meal after working long hours.

So, back to the story.

When Jane enters her home, her AI will be able to predict all the activities that Jane is going to do. This can go further than having an AI for predicting your next grocery list. Jane is feeling cold and her head starts to ache; by nighttime, she starts heating up and starts having dry sweats. Her AI notices that she is not her usual self, thanks to the data gathered from how people behave when they are sick and ill, and alerts all her home appliances of her sickness and what she needs.

The AI checks her temperature and recommends the nearest pharmacy to her home. If Jane wants to go to the pharmacy, the AI will turn on all the lights of the apartment and make sure that she can walk out of her garage safely. Also, her smartphone will automatically receive the information of her needs to go to the pharmacy and call an Uber (or the cheapest and most effective means for transporting) for her to go there.

Smart-system infused medical technology, my other way of calling IoT for MedTech, can add an immense amount of value to patients, from getting their prescriptions for drugs to offering better transparency in the kind of drugs they are taking for their illnesses, not to mention saving time by having a virtual meeting with their doctor for minor sicknesses. I am talking about a world where patients can remotely contact their doctor and receive prescriptions for their medication (given that there will be a smart device that enables doctors to monitor heart rate and check symptoms by using a mix of wearable devices and virtual communication content that streams the patients' sickness in real time).

Through IoT technology, life will be integrated through various devices. We are talking about multiple devices communicating with each other to move in unison to provide the user with more options and convenience by gathering data and analyzing the user's past movements through sensors and the internet. The two biggest areas that we will be seeing an improvement in is in our home and how we get our medicine.

I will be talking more about the potential benefits of what will happen in our lives more specifically in these two parts.

SMART HOME

———

The world is becoming more interconnected via the internet. Well-known information technology industry companies like Samsung, Intel, and IBM are all in this business of fostering interconnection. The details of how they are changing the world will be explained further as we progress through this book. The world is filled with this notion of digital transformation. Working in a company like Samsung, I was able to be more exposed to how technology will be shaping our world and also about the increasing demand for digital connectivity ranging from autonomous vehicles to smart devices in our refrigerators. The world as we all know it will be more connected through technology, and it all starts from the convenience of your home appliances.

When talking about smart homes, where conventional household appliances will be infused with smart technology, I will emphasize on giving illustrations that can help you better grasp how it is changing. In the US, Amazon's Web Services (AWS) is one of the leaders in creating value to the customers by offering services that create a platform for these AI-driven analytics that can be done to further enhance our quality of life. If you go to AWS's website, it explains their ambition in connecting your life for improvement; below is a quote from their website.

"A connected home brings devices and services together for an integrated, autonomous experience that improves a consumer's life. Connected home experiences include everything from voice-controlled lights, house-cleaning robots, machine learning-enabled security cameras, and Wi-Fi routers that troubleshoot for you. Thanks to decreasing costs and increasing options for connectivity, these smart home devices, sensors, and tools can be interlinked to create real-time, contextual, and smart experiences for consumers.

The Internet of Things powers the connected home by bringing new features and capabilities to smart devices, like inter-connectivity, security, offline communication, predictive maintenance, analytics for consumer insights, and machine learning. Each of these capabilities play a different role in key connected home use cases such as home automation, home security and monitoring, and home networking."- excerpt from https://aws. amazon.com/ko/iot/solutions/connected-home/

TURNING YOUR APPLIANCE INTO AN INFORMATION HUB

A smart home, or "connected home" in Amazon's terms, is basically creating a system where your daily chores and home maintenance can be automated. It is freedom from walking into a dark and cold apartment after working late at work, freedom from having to throw out food because you've forgotten that there was milk in your refrigerator for months and it's going sour, freedom from threat of burglary or any kind of unwanted trespassing on your property, freedom from having to turn off the lights when you fall asleep while watching television late at night, and most importantly, freedom from having to make decisions about the tiny details in life that are preventing you from thinking ahead and being productive toward your future.

The Internet of Things is going to offer a liberating feeling to people from the annoying hassles of life. It's an intricate connection of multiple products that is tied into a one giant network where data flows between devices and media to make sure that everything is customized to your needs.

Let's look at our conventional refrigerator; it was for so long the means to store your food longer at a lower temperature. "Refrigeration is an essential food storage technique in developed countries. The lower temperature lowers the reproduction rate of bacteria, so the refrigerator reduces the rate of spoilage."[29]

However, in the eyes of the IoT industry, looking at the refrigerator is more than just a box that is for storing food at a colder temperature. Thanks to technology, refrigerators can be smart. They can be infused with sensors that can control the longevity of certain produce that can have a longer preservation period and be able to help your family with inventory control so that no food will be thrown out because people forgot that they had it in the fridge before it was too late.

If you look at it this way, a refrigerator can be a device that enables tremendous advances in our modern lives, and it should be the centerpiece for innovation and possibly a key item for home improvement in the digital era. I spoke to a former consultant who had worked with many South Korean electronics manufacturers, who wants to remain anonymous, and they said that "Refrigerators are the only devices that are working 24/7. Hence, having a device that is working

---

29   "Refrigerator." Wikipedia. Wikimedia Foundation, May 5, 2019.

24/7 be the center of IoT device connectivity is the logical step towards innovation."

He also mentioned that the 2015 CES was a Kickstarter that got international attention on what IoT is. "CES **(formerly an acronym for** Consumer Electronics Show) is an annual trade show organized by the Consumer Technology Association (CTA). Held in January at the Las Vegas Convention Center in Las Vegas, Nevada, United States, the event typically hosts presentations of new products and technologies in the consumer electronics industry."[30]

IOT IS WHAT, AGAIN? (JUST TO REFRESH YOUR MEMORY)

IoT, the essential technology that will make your home smart, is about creating an ecosystem where every device works together in unison to provide a value and convenience to the users on an unprecedented scale. This proves that digital connectivity will take place in a form of highly diversified devices, all with sensors and chips, for high connectivity, hence making sure that all tasks are automated for the customer's needs.

---

30 "Consumer Electronics Show." Wikipedia. Wikimedia Foundation, April 16, 2019.

The notion of connecting your home for convenience is a business opportunity that a lot of tech companies are getting involved in. In fact, according to statista.com, the smart appliance segment is due to increase in the future with the current market conditions (without any expected boosts expected from higher network connectivity), and already there was a 42.9 percent increase in smart homes and a 38.5 percent increase in revenue for this segment that will total to $21.682 billion generated in 2019.

Jeff Bezos, the founder of Amazon, has been heavily involved in the development of the IoT industry and has said that "For all practical purposes, the market size is unconstrained"[31] in an interview mentioned by thestreet.com. This definitely shows market potential for the IoT and how fast people are adapting to the future.

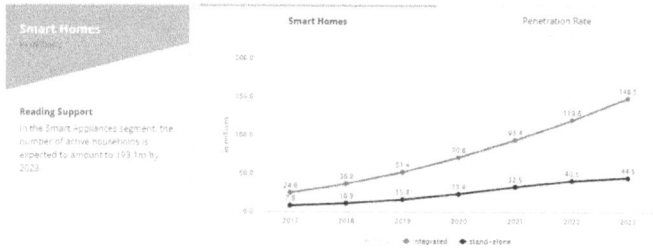

31 Jhonsa, Eric. "Jeff Bezos: Amazon's Market Size Is Effectively Unlimited." TheStreet, September 5, 2018.

The above picture was taken from statista.com[32]

Therefore, it is not an exaggeration to say that smart devices will benefit and bring value to their users. Just imagine your new smart watch and your smartphone being synced with your refrigerator. That refrigerator will work as a hub for your home digital connectivity so that every family member will have access to each other's schedules and post them on the screen in front of the your fridge as a form of blackboard where all your family members can read them in the morning. Also, the list of groceries that needs to be bought can be displayed along with the photos and stories of current events, and announcements of today's to-do list can be posted and shared between your family members in the morning.

If you look it up on the internet, there are very good descriptions of how your refrigerator can be more than just a mere means of preserving food but can also produce a management

---

32 "Smart Appliances - Worldwide | Statista Market Forecast." Statista. Accessed May 9, 2019.

system and a blackboard for all your family members to share every morning before going off to work or school. Below are the steps that the smart home devices (your refrigerator will do) that will make your life more convenient. I was looking over the internet, and livewire.com has the smart refrigerator explained the best as seen in the picture.[33]

Smart Refrigerator Features

While exact features included will vary by brand and model, here is an overview of some of the many things you never knew a fridge could do. Keep in mind, not all smart refrigerators have the same features.

Use the touchscreen interface to:

- Coordinate schedules for every member of the family.
- Look up recipes and have your fridge read the steps while you cook.
- Create grocery lists that sync to your smartphone in real-time.
- Set expiration dates and receive notifications to use food while its fresh.
- Upload photos for display.
- Create individual profiles for each family member to send them personal notes and to-do lists.
- Use a whiteboard option to leave messages for your family.
- Transparent touchscreens allow you to look inside the fridge without opening the door.
- Cast from a smart TV in another room to watch from the kitchen.

The touchscreen is not the only novel thing a smart fridge can do. You can also use your smart fridge features to:

- Customize temperature by drawer or compartment.
- Use interior cameras while at the store to double-check if you're low on milk or eggs.
- Alert you when the water filter needs to be changed.
- Turn the ice maker on or off from your smartphone.

---

33 Midrack, Renée Lynn. "What Is so Smart About a Smart Fridge?" Lifewire. Lifewire, April 30, 2019.

Smart usage of technology in the means of digital connectivity between devices will allow not only higher convenience but also cost savings and efficient use of resources for families. According to an article in *Forbes* magazine, companies that have adapted smart refrigerator technology have saved money by adopting technology into their refrigerators.[34]

I could give another example from an article written by Michael Kanellos, where he said,

"Imagine for a second if you inserted processing power, networking, and memory into dynamic control. Your local utility might offer you a payment—$5 per month, let's say—if your refrigerator promises not to run a defrost cycle between 2 p.m. and 6 p.m. Your frozen burritos won't mind, you won't notice, and your local utility will be able to insulate itself from power spikes on hot summer days. Enlist enough refrigerators and air conditioners, and your utility can contemplate postponing new multimillion-dollar peaker plants. Does it make sense? Are you putting your Hungry Man frozen pot pies at risk? Great Lakes Cold Storage in Pennsylvania has been using dynamic power controls over an 8.6 million cubic foot facility to save $250,000 a year."[35]

34 Kanellos, Michael. "Hold The Laughter: Why The Smart Fridge Is A Great Idea." Forbes. Forbes Magazine, January 13, 2016.
35 Kanellos, Michael. "Hold The Laughter: Why The Smart Fridge Is A Great Idea." Forbes. Forbes Magazine, January 13, 2016.

The picture above is from medium.com[36]

If more and more households utilize the benefits that technology can bring, then they can certainly make their lives be easier in such fast-changing times. Families today already have messaging systems like WhatsApp that can be downloaded for free through the internet and can share their schedules with each other via Google Calendar. If they can incorporate that level of sharing into an existing old appliance in their home by having the medium of a sharing platform that can spread information to all wearable devices that each family member wears (like the glasses that tell you your health status like the ones you see soldiers wearing in sci-fi movies)

36 IronsExpert. "Smart Kitchens a Reality - IOT." Medium. Medium, February 25, 2018.

or a device in your vehicle that makes sure that it is synced in real time. Then there could be more value added to every household by adding productivity. I believe this effect will have a multiplier effect and can increase overall output for the economy and for society in general.

BREAKING AWAY FROM THE
CONVENTIONAL WISDOM

The conventional wisdom of information technology was to focus on a single blockbuster device that was a game changer. I was taught of this wisdom since the first day I started working in tech. From PCs to smartphones, the hardware for the information technology industry is to make a device that will be superior to the existing ones of today with new and improved design and usefulness. I have learned from my mentors at Samsung that the proliferation of the internet in the nineties helped spread the usage of such devices for communication purposes. However, everyone was concentrating on something totally new, something that no one had ever seen or heard of before. What frustrated me was that people weren't concentrating on the synergy effect between devices and how the old incumbent devices could also bring better value to the customer that uses it. Everyone was searching for something very new and was neglecting the benefits that our current appliances had that could be improved.

All that is about to change now with the introduction of wearable devices. People not only want to watch movies and videos on their smartphones but would like to manage their schedules via their smartphone and have it synced to their TVs so that they can easily access their schedule and monitor their messages while watching their favorite reality TV shows.

I once interviewed a sales staff member of a luxury watch company (who wished to remain anonymous). I was interested in engaging in the smartwatch business, so I was asking him about his opinion on smartwatches (this was before the Apple watch and Fitbit came along and changed the dynamics of the wearable industry). He, at that time, which was 2010, thought the market was indisputable and no one could change the dynamics of the watch industry that has been around for more than a century.

This, in my opinion, couldn't have been more wrong. Think about how many people are now wearing smartwatches as their primary tool for telling time. I wish I could go back and tell him to be on alert for what people really wanted. People want a device that is more than just a time piece for a fashion statement. But I guess he now knows the value in infusing technology in watches since many of the old watch makers are now introducing smartwatches to the market.

In an article in *The Wall Street Journal* called "Is Time Running Out for the Swiss Watch Industry?" the article talks about how the Swiss industry is being disrupted by technology companies. The author, Matthew Dalton, writes "The Swiss industry faced a new threat in 2014 when Apple announced its smartwatch, which can display emails, monitor physical activity, and serve as an electronic wallet. Mr. Biver (CEO of Tag Heuer) feared the Apple watch, priced as low as $400, could compete for customers of TAG Heuer's least expensive models, which start at $1,000 and just tell the time."[37]

"Swiss luxury watch brands like TAG Heuer unveiled its $1,500 'connected watch,' which had a step counter and could display emails and run other apps, in November 2015, just months after Apple's smartwatch went on sale."[38]

Technology such as this will cause disruption in the existing market. Introduction of smartphones pretty much dried up any market for flip phones (although I must say I like my Motorola Razr). We've all thought the invention of smartphones replaced these conventional phones because it was cool

37 Dalton, Matthew. "Is Time Running Out for the Swiss Watch
    Industry?" The Wall Street Journal. Dow Jones & Company,
    March 12, 2018.
38 Dalton, Matthew. "Is Time Running Out for the Swiss Watch
    Industry?" The Wall Street Journal. Dow Jones & Company,
    March 12, 2018.

to watch videos on your phone, but now we know that smartphones are here to stay because these devices have introduced a whole new set of possibilities of interconnectivity, that your calendars and your work emails can be mobile in your palm. This digital transformation of your life is what people really wanted, and more and more devices will be introduced that will enable your phones to be connected to your homes and appliances. This is when the old gets revamped and life will be changed for the better on a grander scale.

It's the way of life that if you create something new, the old must wither. For the watch industry, it is not as dramatic since old timepieces still represent the testament of social status and fashionable traits and analog love that people have as their preference, but this new technology that offers a cheaper and multipurpose wearable that not only tells the time but also monitors your health and keeps your email and schedules on check, is the start of what is the Internet of Things that creates digital connectivity that encompasses a synthesis of all your daily activity into a device in a multipurpose and omnipresent way.

BRAIN AND CONNECTIVITY?

The 2019 CES conference did mention that better connectivity is making data transfer easier and will enable computers to make faster and real-time decisions like a human brain. For example, a typical person makes 180 decisions per minute with reaction times of 0.7 to 3 seconds while driving.[39] A 5.8Ghz connection speed will not be able to completely encompass the speed and the multiple decision-making capacity of a human brain. All this will mean that 5G, however, can be a game changer. I will talk more about whether a platform changes the way people create new content in a later chapter, but 5G is important because it will enhance the speed of data transfer and will enable microchips in different devices to interconnect with each other. Also, the microchips can comprehend recommendations made by artificial intelligence like Alexa that can make recommendations based on the user's preference and reaction toward a certain action or an object.

"Amazon's Alexa is a virtual assistant developed by Amazon. com, first used in the Amazon Echo and the Amazon Echo Dot smart speakers developed by Amazon Lab126. It is capable of voice interaction, music playback, making to-do lists, setting alarms, streaming podcasts, playing audiobooks, and providing weather, traffic, sports, and other real-time information, such as news. Alexa can also control several smart devices using itself as a home automation system. Users are able to extend the Alexa capabilities by installing 'skills' (additional functionality developed by third-party vendors, in other

---

39   Pdcteam. "Reaction Time." PoliceDriver.Com, October 29, 2016.

settings more commonly called apps such as weather programs
and audio features)."[40]

Many experts in tech companies agree with my thoughts on this aspect. I have spoken with Georgetown alums that are working at Amazon and also with Ben Edwards, who runs a robotics company called Misty Robotics, that IoT and robotics that use high connectivity coupled with advanced microchips will foster a greater creative impact in the user experience.

TOOL FOR DATA COLLECTION, MAKING DATA BECOME MORE THAN WHAT'S ON THE INTERNET

At Georgetown University McDonough School of Business, we have learned a lot about the implications of these AIs in the business world. However, where does a program that is trained to gather information get its source from? That is where the IoT comes in, and I will delve more deeply into the application of the devices and how it will change and digitally transform our lives as we progress.

Artificial intelligence and the fourth industrial revolution is another topic that I will discuss in the future, but if you just search Alexa (Amazon's AI) online, the applications that this AI can be used for to connect to various different IoT devices

---

40   "Amazon Alexa." Wikipedia. Wikimedia Foundation, May 9, 2019.

for everyday use has endless possibilities. Take a look at how many connectable devices are mentioned on Wikipedia:[41]

Smart home [edit]

- Amazon Dash Wand (2017 version)[130]
- GE Sol LED Lamp[131]
- LG InstaView smart refrigerator[132]
- Nucleus Anywhere Intercom[133]
- Omate Yumi Robot[134],[135]
- ecobee4 smart thermostat[136]
- Ecobee Switch+ light switch[137]
- iDevices Instinct light switch
- First Alert Onelink Safe & Sound smoke alarm and carbon monoxide detector (2018 version)[138]
- Kohler Co. Verdera Voice Lighted Mirror[139]
- Netgear Orbi Voice Wi-Fi router[140]

Wearables and earphones [edit]

- OV by ONvocal headphones[141]
- Lynx robot[142]
- Pebble Core[143] (cancelled due to Fitbit acquisition, product did not reach retail)
- Orion Labs Onyx smart walkie-talkie[144]
- iMCO CoWatch[145]
- Martian mVoice Smartwatches[146]
- Omate Rise Smartwatch[147]
- Bragi Dash and Dash Pro earbuds[148]

Automotive [edit]

- Ford vehicles (select models)[149]
- BMW vehicles (all 2018 models)[150]
- Mini vehicles (all 2018 models)[151]
- Toyota vehicles (select 2018 models)[152]
- Lexus vehicles (select 2018 models)[153]
- Volkswagen vehicles (2018 models)[154]
- Garmin Speak[155]
- Muse by Speak Music[156]
- Roav Viva by Anker[157]

Others [edit]

- Roger (app)[158]
- Voice in a Can app for Apple Watch[159]
- EchoSim (website)[160]
- Amazon iOS and Android shopping apps (only for purchasing products from Amazon.com)[161]

---

41 "Amazon Alexa." Wikipedia. Wikimedia Foundation, May 9, 2019.

The IoT is about connectivity and infusion of these devices into your productivity. It is supposed to be sets of individual devices that are all honed into one giant connectivity. A single device alone is not enough to provide the level of connectivity that a person has in their lives. I mean, you cannot have your phone assess the amount of traffic that is coming your way and track all the goods that you need to buy while being able to manage your heart rate so that you can routinely check your health while doing your weekend activities with your family and friends.

In other words, the IoT devices are sensor-infused devices that you have in your life—your phones, watches, bags, glasses, water bottles, whatever it is, it's going to be smart! And of the sensors needed for this technology, none are more advanced than the sensors you see in elevators. And every device is connected to the internet, which means that sensor technology in hardware and advanced networks can channel the data gathered by the individual with a software platform that is powerful enough to encompass massive amounts of data and allow companies, organizations, and governments to turn that data into intelligence.

LIMITS OF HUMAN BEINGS AND NEED FOR INFRASTRUCTURE TO MOVE BEYOND HOME

Human beings are not capable of deciphering mass data into usable intelligence. The book *Prediction Machines* by Ajay Agrawal, Joshua Gans, and Avi Goldfarb explains these aspects better:

"Machines and humans have distinct strengths and weaknesses in the context of prediction. As prediction machines improve, businesses must adjust their division of labor between humans and machines in response. Prediction machines are better than humans at factoring in complex interactions among different indicators, especially in settings with rich data."

"As number of dimensions for such interactions grows, the ability of humans to form accurate predictions diminishes, especially relative to machines." (page 69)

The book later stresses the need for collaboration between humans and machines where humans have strength in the unknown factors and should pivot their business strategy to work by incorporating the machine's fast learning curve with the human element.

The more in-depth knowledge about AI and machine learning is a whole new set of topics that deserves much deeper attention and professional studies, but the IoT industry cannot survive without such machine brains that can turn data gathered from these devices into intelligence for strategy. The industrial revolution coming from sensors, network, and AI is happening on a large scale. The book talks about how changes can happen in the devices by using sensors in municipal and manufacturing.

On May 16, 2019, I was at an event held at the Center for Strategic and International Studies (CSIS) called "America's Global Infrastructure Opportunity: Three Recommendations to the New US Development Finance Corporation" from 1:00 p.m. to 3:00 p.m. "The event was about gathering professionals from Working Group on US Development Finance for Infrastructure to consider the context and emerging opportunities and provide focused recommendations. The panel was professionals with in-depth knowledge about growth and infrastructure, and what I heard in that session was very riveting."[42]

The key idea from the event was that investment in developing emerging markets be done around smart cities. I will be explaining more about smart cities in the next chapters,

---

42 Thursday, May 16. "America's Global Infrastructure Opportunity: Three Recommendations to the New U.S. Development Finance Corporation." America's Global Infrastructure Opportunity: Three Recommendations to the New U.S. Development Finance Corporation | Center for Strategic and International Studies, October 12, 2018.

but it's a city that uses technology to create solutions that improve people's lives.

In the future, whoever has data will have a competitive edge to lead the world. Cities should realize that using technology to solve problems is a key strength. For example, they use technology by using patterns of how people are moving around and make sure that security and public transportation are available for people's lives to be more efficient. Such devices are available through the IoT devices that are being used in homes and lives. I will be talking more about how this technology will not only be enhancing people's private homes but also public goods that will enable productivity and convenience.

CARS COMMUNICATING WITH EACH OTHER AND READING THE ROAD FOR US

The connected car concept itself is self-explanatory. It's basically connecting your car with other vehicles on the roads. This will enable cars to detect each other's speed and movements so that the car will alert the driver about the potential danger that a driver can incur in the intersections. Car crashes in intersections happen quite frequently; I was personally involved in a car accident when I was driving in an intersection. I thought I was being careful with my driving, but my insurance agent told me that there are aspects of the human mind that cause errors that make us cause this accident to happen quite often. So when I heard about the safety technologies that companies like Tesla and other automotive car companies were talking about that will make cars potentially communicate with each other to enhance driver safety, I was very interested. I was at a Tesla dealership and was speaking with a sales rep there, and he said that this technology is already present and that cars that are made recently already have such mechanisms that enhance driver safety.

If you take a visit to your local dealership for any of the car brands that are out there in the market, all of their latest cars are packed with technology for driver safety. Options like forward collision warning and active safety measures like automatic braking systems can be bought. It's amazing how the automotive industry is using these technologies to enhance safety. Already, I am seeing IoT technology being infused in our lives that enable cars to use radio waves via sensors and cameras to warn drivers of potential car accidents through countless analyses of traffic patterns and on-the-road data and communications between vehicles.

To further educate myself on this aspect of how IoT can save lives and improve safety for drivers, I attended the ITS America 28th Annual Meeting of Intelligent Mobility: Safer. Greener. Smarter held at the Walter E. Washington

Convention Center from June 4 to June 7, 2019. I was participating in a session where they talked about a Cross-industry Perspective on Connected, Safer Transportation. The session consisted of leaders from government agencies, automotive, and technology sectors that are working together to bring safety through technology.

I was very impressed with the level of concern and forward thinking these panels had, and they talked about connectivity between cars as the foundation of how we can share information on how we can make roads safer for drivers. Like my car accident, much of the collisions happen due to human errors, and much of the car accidents that are caused by humans can be avoided if cars are connected to monitor movement and speed to alert the driver of the potential dangers lurking near the blind spots that are not visible with the human eye.

What the panel stated in this session was the same as my thoughts about how this can all work. The technology is already available: sensor technology and advanced connectivity and software development is available today. But the key problem is to figure out combining them across multiple public and private sectors; this is the key in bringing this to fruition. When you are talking about connected cars, you're talking about involving a lot of people from different sectors that have never worked together before. If a car is to be connected, you first need the cars to be packed with technology that enables them to be connected to the internet that can process real-time information to alert the drivers.

If the cars are capable for connectivity, then the cars need roads that are paved with enough bandwidth power that can have multiple cars to be connected at once that can deliver enough information so that there will be no lags in how the road information is being processed. This means that government agencies in the transportation and infrastructure sectors, car companies, and telecom companies as well as software (AI and cloud) and data processing companies all need to work in unison. Combining all of these players together will be an ensemble cast that will need a lot of organization and planning power that has never been done before.

These industries work in different time frames of innovation (chip makers and car companies work in different time frames for developing new models) and also basically speak different languages when it comes to the knowledge of introducing new products to the market. There must be an enterprise or an entity that can understand the differences and devise a framework that can work for both the private and public sectors.

I've also spoken with a lot of people who are involved in the sector, and they said that car connectivity can happen ten years from now. I find this very fascinating because increased safety will enable greater access of mobility for people, which will increase economic activities. However, if this is to happen, every professional I talked to about this matter stressed the fact that organization is the biggest priority, and also how well the combined efforts across industries and government will bring the future to us will evidently determine how fast this technology will be deployable in the future.

MAKING ALL DEVICES AND VEHICLES SMART

On March 13, there was a *Wall Street Journal* article that said companies are investing in this technology very seriously. That article, titled "SoftBank, Other Investors in Talks to Invest $1 Billion in Uber's Self-Driving Unit," talks about how serious companies are trying to take advantage of this new technology. The article also mentions that

"Uber has struck other investment deals that double as strategic partnerships and are aimed at lowering development costs and containing losses in its autonomous-vehicle unit. Last year, Toyota Motor Corp. announced plans to invest about $500 million in Uber as part of an agreement to work jointly on

self-driving cars. Toyota's investment valued Uber at about $72 billion."[43]

The way such technology works is about how sensors are used to receive data from many vehicles and devices and use artificial intelligence to make analysis. There are other examples of this technology as well. Much of the technology for the wearable market is happening in the MedTech industry, where IDC projects by year 2020 the market capitalization for the MedTech wearable industry is projected to be $515 billion.[44] To put it into a better perspective, the world's steel industry is worth $900 billion.[45] I will be talking more about MedTech in the upcoming chapters in this part, but yes, it's big, and it will be a gargantuan upgrade in our lives.

So, we are talking about an industry where IoT will play a major role that is worth more than half of the world's steel consumption. MedTech is one example where fast connectivity will have the biggest impact, and I have designated a chapter that explains further about how MedTech and IoT will create business opportunities in the future. But in

43   Farrell, Maureen. "SoftBank, Other Investors in Talks to Invest $1 Billion in Uber's Self-Driving Unit." The Wall Street Journal. Dow Jones & Company, March 13, 2019.

44   Zogbi, Dennis M. "The Global Market for Medical Electronics and Outlook to 2022."TTI, February 28, 2017.

45   Angel, Maytaal. "Worldsteel Raises Forecast for 2018 Global Steel Demand Growth to..." Reuters. Thomson Reuters, April 17, 2018.

this chapter, I would like to focus on how 5G will enable a faster network to travel fast and how this can create more opportunity.[46]

SO, HOW WILL THIS IMPACT OUR FUTURE LIKE THE BOOK SAYS IN 2030?

I have talked about infrastructure projects and how this could lay out the platform for cool things like smart vehicles that will drive themselves and also recommend your destination depending on your daily needs that are captured through countless sensors and recognition devices that will be implanted all over your lives.

I strongly believe that people will be more likely to demand a watch with connectivity functions as the IoT industry flourishes. I mean, having a watch that syncs to your refrigerator to alert you to needed grocery lists and at the same time can text your family while you are commuting in a packed subway during rush hour without having to whip out your phone all the time is pretty cool and handy.

This demand will also explode and grow exponentially with the introduction of faster means of connectivity such as 5G; this concept will be expanded to your vehicles and home

---

46 Zomorodi, Behsad. "How Do Clinical Wearables Impact Patient Care and Quality of Life?" Healthcare IT News, June 16, 2018.

electronics to a wireless platform. The devices will have a higher rate than the standard connectivity that we have in 4G, and it will enable fast data transfers. The new platform for better transfers can create opportunity in flows of information from mere data transfer to a more qualitative decision-making. In my conversation with Professor JeongGil Ko, then of Ajou University, such a platform can create rooms for innovation where software can process and receive enough information to enable machine learning. The 2019 CES also proved Professor Ko's argument that the world is now focusing on artificial intelligence to analyze people's preferences and decisions can be made for them.[47]

47   Carter, Jamie. "CES 2019: All the Latest News and Reviews." TechRadar. TechRadar, January 11, 2019.

MEDTECH

———

The ability to check your health has always been either expensive or time-consuming. When I need a health checkup, I have to go to a designated lab for blood testing or a hospital to measure my blood pressure. Both activities take time and cost a lot of money. We have talked about sensors being the key component that makes the IoT industry able to make our lives more convenient by tracking our movements and our needs; we can do this for our health as well. Medical technology (or MedTech) is an area that is growing rapidly, and I would like to talk about the fascinating changes that are evolving around infusing the IoT into our health care to make health tracking more affordable and easier for people to use.

MedTech, or ubiquitous health care according to International Review of Information Ethics, "is an emerging area of technology that uses a large number of environmental and patient sensors and actuators to monitor and improve patients' physical and mental condition."[48] Ubiquitous health care is one of the fields that is growing for the usage of IoT devices. In my conversation with Professor Ko, he stressed that such MedTech industry is growing rapidly as healthcare practitioners continue to adopt new technologies and connectivity to advance patient care. Electronic MedTech devices are diverse and include assisting devices (like hearing aids, pacemakers, and pad-mounted displays for people in wheelchairs), imaging devices, and monitoring devices, among others.

Just imagine doctors speaking with their patients online and giving them feedback via data collected from these wearable health-care devices that are armed with sensors to measure and transfer data to the doctors in real time. A clear diagnosis of the symptoms patients have would need high connectivity, if you think about the amount of distance there will be from the patient's home to where the doctors are. However, what we also need to acknowledge is that the user experience has to be friendly enough for patients to feel comfortable talking

---

48 Brown, Ian, and Andrew A Adams. "The Ethical Challenges of Ubiquitous Healthcare." International review of information Ethics, December 2017.

to their doctors as if they are in front of you from afar. Speed of transmitting information (which will happen thanks to 5G being deployed all over the world) is not enough to make this happen. Content and devices that track your daily heart rate and status should also be created to make sure that patients and doctors can communicate virtually.

I have mentioned the amount of abundant resources being invested in this effort by the amount of money that is being invested into the MedTech development, if you see the below table made by statista.com.[49]

Worldwide medtech research and development spending as percent of medtech revenue from 2011 to 2024

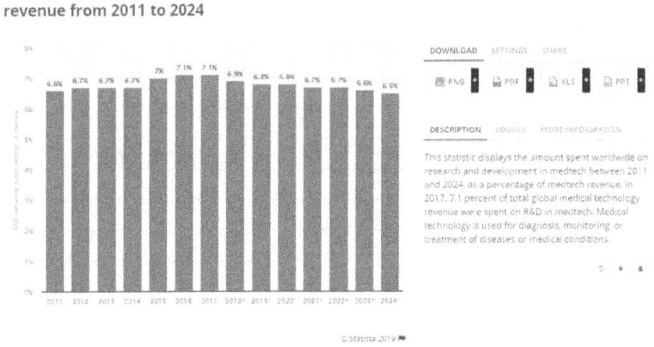

It is evident that the MedTech industry is growing; you hear a lot of stories in the news about how the population is aging, and the need for affordable health care has been one of the

49   "Global Medtech R&D Spending Medtech Revenue Share 2011-2024 | Statistic." Statista. Accessed May 23, 2019.

key social problems that needs to be addressed in the future. And it brings me to ponder what it would be like if you could infuse the IoT devices and connectivity together.

The thing I love about business is that there is always a way to bring the most value to users and customers. There is always a problem to solve, and the best businesses are the ones that can identify this problem and deliver a service that can solve this complication and opaqueness and create value for the public.

So, what if there is a service out there that offers contents and devices that can provide a service for those who want to visit the doctor's office but are too busy or cannot walk to the hospital? What if you've visited your doctors and would like a quick second opinion to reassure you that you are indeed okay? Also, what if you are prescribed a certain medicine, but you want to make sure that it's safe for you?

These are all questions that people I have talked with who frequently visit the hospital have told me when I asked them how the medical industry could do better. It's highly likely that such questions are in high demand for a solution and that it is equally very hard to find.

Let's face it, a general search in Google doesn't really give you much information about when your medication is made up of and who is distributing it in what manner. Not to mention the fact that it's equally hard to find out how good your doctor is and where to find the best doctors for your medical treatment. Anyone can tell that there is lack of transparency in the medical industry. For example, my wife had an allergic reaction last winter (2018); however, we couldn't figure out what the real reason was that caused the symptoms. We visited multiple medical institutions: first, we visited a doctor that our friend recommended; then, the doctor recommended us to an allergist, and the allergist then gave us the go sign to get allergy testing at a designated lab.

The time span of this process took almost three weeks from making appointments to finding time to physically get to the doctors, which was a thirty-minute drive from our home, and to make reservations at the lab near where we live near DC. Imagine if this can be shortened because you no longer have to wait in line at the hospital because your AI has set up an appointment when you recorded your symptoms online through your smartphone, and you no longer have to physically go to the doctor's office because you have devices at home that can connect you to the doctor virtually (and relay all the necessary insurance information beforehand) and take blood samples at home and make reservations for your next appointment automatically.

Health is directly related to your well-being, probably the most necessary to your well-being. But why is it that we can find better information on the composition of your T-shirt than your sickness and your doctor's competency and the medication you are taking? My hope is that information sharing through such connectivity will bring transparency into people's health and medication.

VIRTUAL DOCTORS

While I was learning about virtual reality and how this can be used to improve people's lives, I was able to speak with people that were working on virtual medical devices. The person that I spoke with no longer works in this field, but when I was speaking with him in 2017, he let me know about the fascinating future of medical technology and virtual reality. However, the services were limited due to the limitations on the connectivity and the devices that are not interoperable from this lack of connectivity methods. The kinds of services that a doctor can bring to their patients online can be done with the current 4G technology; however, if the doctor is supposed to give feedback in order to diagnose their patients in real time via wireless, then the story is different using the current LT or 4G: the technology is too slow for such services to come to fruition.

Health is directly related to our well-being, so there cannot be an acceptable margin of error in diagnosing a person's illness. We have had countless cases where technology was mal-equipped for medical treatment and caused more harm than good. Hence, there must be speed and sufficient contents that can increase the accuracy of the sensors so that ubiquitous health care could be possible. A patient should be able to connect with the doctor as if he or she is right in front of the patient analyzing the current symptoms and assuring the patient with high-quality resolution to make sure that any swollen part of the body is represented correctly. The current 4G technology lacks in its delivery; hence, the content of the MedTech should be coupled with the high connectivity of 5G to ensure a true ubiquitous user experience.[50]

50 Zomorodi, Behsad. "How Do Clinical Wearables Impact Patient Care and Quality of Life?" Healthcare IT News, June 16, 2018.

Many health-care companies are trying to consolidate their businesses to offer a service that is much like what a virtual doctor will offer through the internet. For example, "Royal Philips has signed an agreement to acquire Carestream Health's health-care information systems (HCIS) business unit. Carestream's HCIS business unit includes enterprise imaging IT solutions for multisite hospitals, radiology services providers, imaging centers, and specialty medical clinics."[51] The services will provide medical consultation online with image-related treatment results, but real-time diagnoses like checking your pulse need a much faster connectivity that can transfer data in real time from patient to doctor.

FINDING A DOCTOR THAT FITS

Let's think of a scenario where this will all work. Let's say that you woke up with a very bad stomachache and couldn't move a muscle from your bed. You begin to track back your memories as if you're rewinding a cassette tape (yes, this used to be a thing in the nineties). You start by what you ate for breakfast to the small snacks you've had in between meals. Even if you do suspect something you've ate that might have gone bad, you will want to ask your doctor what went wrong and what kind of medication you need to take for this pain to go away. Now, if you live near a hospital, this won't be a

---

51   Pennic, Fred. "Philips to Acquire Carestream Health's Health IT Business Unit." Healthcare IT News, March 11, 2019.

problem, but if you live in a place where the nearest hospital is at least thirty minutes away by car, driving to see your doctor and back with your condition is out of the question.

But what if there could be a smart tracking device that could measure your heart rate, and you have high resolution cameras and a connectivity platform that could transfer this data to your doctor to see any swellings that could allow you to receive prescriptions in real time for an illness that doesn't necessarily require any blood tests?

The doctor can ask for your symptoms and offer you a prescription that you can print out at your home to take to your pharmacy. Once the prescription is sent from your doctor, the artificial intelligence (a much-matured version of your Alexa or Cortana or Siri) will try to make sure that such medication has been taken by patients with similar symptoms and also provide you with a comprehensive review of users who have used the medicine or been speaking with the doctor you have just spoken with. And if you feel that you need a second opinion on this matter, your artificial intelligence will direct you to another doctor's appointment and can compare what the doctor has to say with the same kind of symptoms you suffer from.

After you are content with your virtual doctors' opinion and the prescriptions, the artificial intelligence will recommend you the nearest pharmacy that provides you the needed medication. Once you have selected the pharmacy you want to go to, the artificial intelligence will store this preference and share it with all your wearable devices (your phones, your watches, your car navigation, etc.), provide the fastest route to take on your navigation (whether it be in your car, on your wrist, or on your phone). Of course, if you are too sick to move, your device will be alert to your dire condition and can call an ambulance or an Uber so that you can get to your hospital/pharmacy as conveniently as possible.

The aforementioned "what if" scenario is possible if there can be a faster connectivity speed, beyond what 4G can offer, due to its faster need for real-time data sharing and also content that can allow the information to be effectively passed from the patient to multiple devices to the hospital. For example, I was talking to my doctor in Korea over the phone, but even if we video chatted, the resolution and the technology was not sophisticated enough to effectively diagnose and also come up with a course of action by operating devices and the patient's needs. Such procedural activities can be done through algorithms, but content must be present to make sure that this can take place flawlessly.

It will be like making an Excel function to calculate the optimal revenue through your solver, but it's more intricately done and on a grander scale to make sure that human lives are impacted positively. I do not know if the infrastructure that provides the speed needs to come before the content or vice versa, but I do know that sensors and wearable devices that require such technology already exist. We have companies like Fitbit that have devices that monitor your heart rate on a regular basis; this is a powerful tool that is already being used with the current technology.

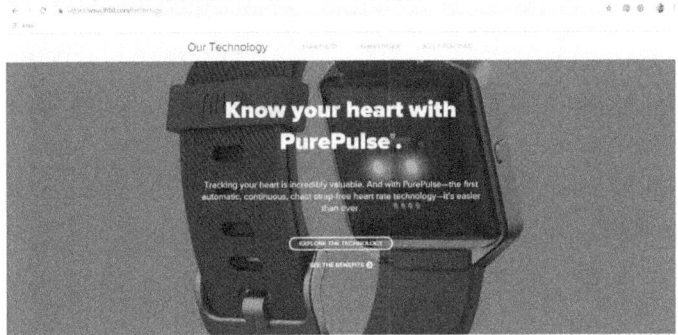

Picture taken from: https://www.fitbit.com/technology

The question is how can we transfer the data the right way so that doctors can see your health status in real time to make virtual meetings possible. Such preventative measures are crucial in ways that can save lives before anything critical happens where people have to send their loved ones away too soon. All it needs is a tipping point for this to happen; I am very positive that patients will be able to see their doctors faster from their homes and will be able to share their opinion about doctors and their prescription medication to make things more transparent for what goes into their bodies to heal their illnesses.

KNOWING YOUR MEDICINE

If you have seen the Netflix documentary series *Dirty Money*, there is an episode called "Drug Short" where they expose drug companies such as Valeant that used malicious business practices such as increasing their revenue through astronomically increasing prices of certain medications. When I saw this documentary, I thought, why is it that I must find out about companies fiddling with people's health on a documentary? I believe looking up your medication should be as easy as looking up the cheapest airfares on Google. If you want the cheapest flight information or to find the best hotel in New York, Google offers you all the ratings of the hotels and prices for the flights available on the days you want to travel.

This is possible because people have a platform and the content to share their knowledge and experience via the internet and book their flights through their devices (may it be a laptop, tablet, or a smart phone). The technology for making the devices for sharing the information is already here. I have seen components that exist in this world that have the sensor capabilities to carry out the needs for what IoT devices should do. However, the content that allows patients to share their medication and use them as reference when they are seeing their doctors is not.

If a wearable device that can analyze your illness and transmit the results to hospitals for a quick diagnosis and share the patient experience on a platform like Google for illnesses, then the public will be more aware of what kind of sickness they have and the kind of medication that is available for doctors to prescribe. This can also work to track the prices and the side effects as well, so when a patient receives a prescription from their doctor, they can immediately check if the medicine has any problems for people with similar symptoms and look up if there are any safer alternatives to their current prescription.

ISSUE WITH IMPLANTED MEDICAL DEVICES

From the acclaimed documentary by Netflix called *The Bleeding Edge*, the medical device market is a huge business—a $300 billion-a-year business. It seems like the medical industry predicts that by 2050 there could be a micro laboratory implanted in our bodies that predicts illnesses before anyone gets sick, and there will be 3D printers that create custom biomechanical organs; also, the advent of AIs can create models for individuals that can predict a person's health and their likelihood of having a heart attack. This all sounds like a marvelous world.

The impact that devices will have on medical care is endless. Innovation, when unleashed properly, can be a way for us to evolve into better beings. The documentary also mentions that medical devices are already a way of life in postindustrial society. It's very prevalent; a lot of devices are saving lives. However, there are cases where such an array of devices being poured into the market can be harmful.

The Bleeding Edge[52] also mentions a fascinating statistic in their introduction that over 70 million Americans have been implanted with medical devices. My grandmother used to have a tracker that kept her heartbeat in check. However, the devices can cause people more harm than good. The documentary made a statement that devices like Essure, a device which was supposed to be an innovative way of birth control, caused twelve thousand adverse events in 2017 to women, and they are terminally injured and need a plethora of medical procedures. Since technology is moving at a phenomenal speed, there needs to be better connectivity within devices to make sure that people are more aware and knowledgeable regarding what is going to be implanted in their bodies.[53]

Making medical devices that are capable of tracking and making recommendations and connecting with the doctors

52 "The Bleeding Edge." Wikipedia. Wikimedia Foundation, April 19, 2019.
53 "The Bleeding Edge." Netflix Official Site, July 27, 2018.

online will be a much better way for users to be informed about the kind of medical treatment there is for their illness when they are in immediate need of prescription medication. For example, an average working mom with three children has spent enough time with her family, and now she wants to put her career higher up in her priorities. This is a typical demand for birth control. However, with the lack of knowledge that she has without any means to retrieve reliable data, she might get swindled by the sales tactic by a medical company and try a clinically untested device or medication that can wind up causing a medical incident.

With digital connectivity in the future, the mother of three might already have a wearable device that can inform her about the clinical trial results of the medicine that the doctor prescribes for her children. This will be possible for her because the artificial intelligence in her wearable recognized the type of medical treatment that the doctor was talking about and conducted a search for her while she was talking to the doctor. This is possible because in a world of digital connectivity, a wearable device has the power to connect with any information that is running in a cloud platform; as I mentioned in my previous chapter about cloud computing, as more people migrate to it, this could be a solution for storing information.

Also, such connectivity and transformation can pave the way for sensor technology to be implanted in medical devices for the human body (implants, and yes, this will take years and years of clinical trials) in the future so that clinical trial data can be uploaded to servers in real time so that anyone who has access to the internet can view the clinical trial data without having to ask for the results from corporations themselves.

Medical devices are dangerous because people are not aware of their safety related to having these in their bodies without being sufficiently informed. This only lets them to only trust the words of the people that are selling the product for revenue. If information can be shared faster and more directly with the customers, with a knowledge and information that can be uploaded and shared in real time, IoT devices will be the medium that can make bring that into fruition.

WHERE MBAS AND BUSINESS PROFESSIONALS ARE THINKING OF MEDICAL TECHNOLOGY

During my first year in my MBA program at Georgetown University in 2019, we had a case study where we recommend a strategic recommendation for a Swiss watch company. My teammates: Yazan Al-Ghabra, Broderick Brown, Lily Siegman, and Erika Wohl, who I had the utmost respect for and pleasure working with, had recommended a Swiss watchmaker to enter the MedTech Industry for patients in hospitals.

The way we presented this case was that in order for businesses to have a long-term competitive advantage, the watchmakers should enter the medical wearable (MedTech) industry. This could happen through multiple ways, but our recommendation was the acquisition of one of the leading wearable makers in the market. When we calculated the valuations of and estimated to synergy that a timekeeper will bring to keeping people's lives in check, it was a priceless value that could be offered to millions of people worldwide.

It was surely a winner, and it was evident that our case was strong that this mega IoT company would save lives and make hospital operations much better. (We did get very good feedbacks on our project, for sure!)

Finding the logical explanation for this business strategy was simple:

1. The MedTech industry is growing rapidly as health-care practitioners continue to adopt new technologies, AI, and connectivity to advance patient care.
2. Electronic MedTech devices are diverse and include assisting devices (like hearing aids and pacemakers), imaging devices, and monitoring devices, among others.

3. The industry is projected to be $515 billion by 2022. There are ample opportunities for growth.

We also found out that the advancement of medical wearables to date, while growing through several start-up companies, has been quite limited. Wearable manufacturers have largely targeted consumer markets with devices that provide continuous monitoring of vitals such as heart rate and fitness activities. Despite popularity within the consumer market, a comprehensive wrist-monitoring wearable has yet to be introduced within the medical wearable industry. This was strange; how could this technology that could be more useful to doctors only be prevalent for daily uses only?

To fill this void, this new MedTech device we envisioned would focus on actively monitoring Emergency Department (ED) patients' vitals including heart rate, body temperatures, and O2 saturation. This device will not only replace initial intake bands with patient information (name, date of birth, etc.) but will also allow for continuous monitoring of patients' health rather than sporadic spot checks by a nurse. We believed this would ultimately increase efficiency and add value to hospitals as a leader in high accuracy and precision tracking.

Figure 1: Global MedTech Market Growth 2005-2016, 2017-2022 Forecasts

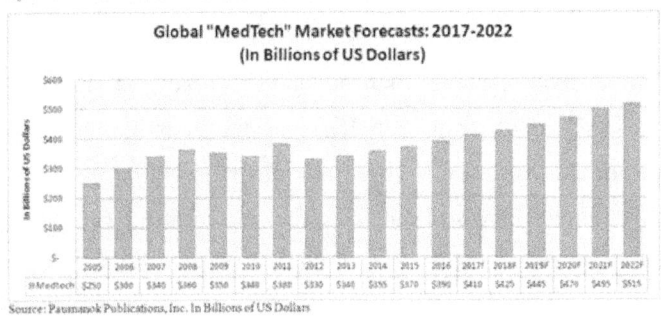

Global "MedTech" Market Forecasts: 2017-2022
(In Billions of US Dollars)

	2005	2006	2007	2008	2009	2010	2011	2012	2013	2014	2015	2016	2017F	2018F	2019F	2020F	2021F	2022F
MedTech	$250	$300	$340	$360	$350	$440	$400	$330	$360	$355	$370	$390	$410	$425	$445	$470	$495	$515

Source: Pausmanok Publications, Inc. In Billions of US Dollars

This project received good feedback from our professors and our classmates, and it was some of my finest work we've accomplished. I met an awesome team that enabled us to think outside the box and think of ways where old can meet new and create a mega-IoT company that helps people's lives be better.

Hence, when IoT moves into medical care, it's not just doctors and scientists and R&D experts that can make changes. I believe there is a business opportunity that can bring value through thinking outside of the norm. This is what my MBA experience has taught me, and it has surely affected me to write more about the things that catapulted me to dedicate so much time to thinking more about how I can help people as a business professional.

SO, HOW WILL THIS IMPACT OUR FUTURE LIKE THE BOOK SAYS IN 2030?

I am a strong believer that medical technology should be at the forefront of innovation. It's what should drive companies to put their money in the most and where all enterprises throughout the world should be focused creating ways to put people's lives healthier. Because let's face it, the longer we live well and affluently, the longer we can spend and consume, which drives the economy to be vibrant and robust.

I understand that medical technology is hard to make and that entering a business that has a direct impact on human lives requires years of development and testing for it to become a marketable product for the consumer market. But it's also where businesses can drive the most value that they create and save lives. Medical businesses should never be about just short-term profits. They should be focusing on the long-term aspects and putting in the work and money so that people can live fruitful lives.

However, whenever I see medical incidents like those I saw in *The Bleeding Edge*, it upsets me that medical technology is harming people's lives instead of saving them. IoT should have a massive role in reversing some of the prejudices that the medical industry has put on the public and mass media and prove that devices can be trusted and can be used for people's well-being.

Using sensor technology and fast connectivity, the possibilities are endless, and it can disrupt the oldest method of Medicare we know today. Patients don't have to set up appointments when they can virtually see their doctors for minor sickness, and doctors should also have the versatility to embrace this sensor technology so that they can monitor their patients more effectively.

PART 3

AT WORK

Let's take a visit to Jane's life again. Let's imagine that she is working at a company that manufactures and delivers super ergonomically friendly wooden chairs to retailers like Walmart and Target (Sure, she could have worked in companies like Tesla or IKEA, but the café I am sitting in to write my book has awesomely comfortable chairs, so that's how my imaginary character got her job in this company.). She works at an operations center, where she and her coworkers are monitoring every detail of the manufacturing procedures, all the way from raw material inputs to delivery of finished goods to the customers.

Normally, this would be impossible to monitor because that means Jane's company needs to have entirely real-time information on what is happening to each product in the supply chain to monitor everything. In case you are not sure of what supply chains are, supply chains are simply the chain of supply of goods that are needed to assemble or manufacture the goods that you are making. So, if her company is making wooden chairs, the company would need to buy raw materials like good quality wood and other components that would be used in making chairs. Hence, orders must be made, and deliveries have to happen prior to what Jane's company has planned for running the manufacturing line to produce them.

Since the agreement for delivery of such raw materials happened through contracts and word of mouth, the production can be vulnerable to all sorts of setbacks from delays from the raw-material producers or receiving bad-quality goods from suppliers. However, all this has changed in Jane's company since the company has made their entire operations smart.

Jane's company has incorporated IoT devices into every manufacturing process in their supply chain. This means that from her control room, Jane will be able to monitor the process of the raw materials being made at their suppliers, since the trucks that deliver the wood have sensors that indicate their whereabouts in real time. These delivery trucks have motion sensors and humidity monitors as well so that Jane will be able to verify that the materials are not harmed when being transported. The trucks are able to use the sensors and transmit data in real time because there is a sufficient infrastructure program for connectivity. This empowered Jane and her company to use these sensors on trucks that are driving on public roads.

Jane can predict the production planning in comparison to the demand for the chairs more accurately. This will enable Jane to encompass more flexibility to plan ahead and to also make sure that every piece of equipment in their manufacturing plant is operating to its full potential once the raw materials have arrived and are loaded onto the conveyor belt (like the Henry Ford manufacturing plant videos we watched when we were in middle school). Also, Jane can immediately determine which processes need more manpower by seeing the schedules of completion for each production phase.

Also, each piece of equipment has data on how much raw material was used for production and how much raw material it threw away to make this product as well (all this can be monitored by floor operators who share information with the command center that Jane is working in), so if a certain piece equipment of in the production phase is using up more raw material than expected, Jane can flag this to the floor engineers to create an improvement plan that can save tremendous amounts of raw material in the future.

The floor operators are also working in a better environment because of the smart factory system because the equipment that they are working with has sensors that identify every worker, and the mechanic arms in the equipment help the operators with lifting materials to the production line and also help them with inspecting the quality of the production after each phase by scanning the production and telling the operators and also the command center (where Jane is working) if they sense an anomaly in the production line.

If there is a quality problem, Jane can immediately alert the quality team about the problem in the production line so that they can make adjustments to the production line, if necessary, in the fastest time possible, while diverting production quickly to other equipment that is producing sound products. Such flexible and smooth operations are not only causing production to be more efficient and effective but is a competitive advantage for Jane's company with their customers because their customers can also see how the products are being produced and be informed of any problems and foreseeable delays in real time. Also, this can help their customers with their retail strategy, which will create room for the customers as well to create even more accurate forecasts for future sales. Therefore, Jane's company can control production cycles and make sure that every piece of equipment is working to its full potential every day.

We all wish we could predict the future better because it's safer, and if it's safer, chances are that you will incur less costs from accidents or mishaps along the way. Business is just the same, but on a massive scale. Being able to predict the problems ahead by having real-time data across your entire production cycle and having it shared with your customers and suppliers; will not only bring trust into the business but also cost-saving opportunities that can increase chances of making a better product and services to customers all over the world. There is nothing but benefits from this phenomenon.

From the smart factory that has been implemented, Jane has more flexibility with her time as well. Before, she used to come to work in the morning and find out that the entire production was delayed the day before it was due to ship out (when this problem was apparent since the first week of production, but the engineers and operators missed inspecting the equipment status correctly). Her life was filled with unwanted surprises, and that caused her to spend late nights trying to figure out the best course of action for her customers, who had no idea that the chars they ordered were going to be delayed by three weeks and had planned a grand opening of their retail stores. Her life was miserable, and she couldn't leave the office without some kind of anxiety or a mistrust of the floor operators. And if problems did happen, it was already too late to solve it, so she had to take the heat from the marketing and sales team that now had to tell the customers that their order that was due tomorrow will be delayed by a month.

But now that her company is infused with smart factory technology, she can see that every production is on time before she leaves work and also can immediately know if there is a problem with the operations in real time, which gives her the time to react and fix the issue or notify the people in her chain immediately to mitigate any negative effects that this can cause to customers and consumers. Yes, Jane is hooked into the system of monitoring the production process 24/7, but she has gained the level of confidence and flexibility in her life to plan ahead and work in a much more predictable environment than before.

However, since a lot of what we consider real-time data is being transferred so fast and so much through the internet, Jane and her colleagues start to worry about the potential breach of privacy at work and also the dangers of information being leaked to unwanted third parties. I cannot stress how important this part is to the age of digital connectivity that we will be embracing: think about how any employee can get monitored from every floor operation 24/7. This can come up with all sorts of ways to improve productivity but also can raise privacy concerns if a floor operator is taking a break or is on his or her cell phone and not paying attention at work.

Privacy is certainly is an issue, but what Jane is most concerned about is her company's system being open for hacking. Since the entire operations platform is up on the internet for real-time monitoring and analysis, a skilled hacker can easily breach the system and get secrets of the company's manufacturing knowledge and its sales projections and sell them to its competitor, which can eradicate the years of hard work that Jane and her coworkers had built for decades.

However, Jane is in safe hands because her CEO had just hired a chief technology officer (CTO) in her company that oversees all security measures so that data and information gathered by Jane's operation center does not get into the wrong hands; for example, a third party data mining company that sells people's information for profits. Also, the CEO and the head of human resources are also aware of the fact that the information gathered on the operations floor will in no way be used to monitor people's whereabouts or use it to breach any kind of privacy that can harm people that work for this company. Jane is relieved that her company has embraced technology that makes her work life so much more convenient and effective and safe.

She remembers how technology was only for companies that were dubbed "tech companies" or banks that had money to implement such hip systems and not conventional manufacturers like her chair manufacturing company. IoT has crumbled the barriers of who gets to use technology to be more efficient and effective in operating a business, and she hopes that this technology can proliferate into small businesses as well, where local bakeries can use these affordable sensors to make effective store management possible to save on costs and boost product quality.

Technology can bring tremendous efficiency and innovation at work, but if it is used by wrong people with wrong agendas, Jane fears that this can incur some serious damage if this data gets breached by hackers or any cyberterrorists out there. Therefore, as much as IoT will enhance data gathering and data analytics to make people's lives more efficient, it also opens doors for threats that have not been dealt with in modern manufacturing, retail, or any other consumer-centric businesses.

Jane's life seems like light years away, but if you go on YouTube and look up how companies like Boeing and Tesla is making their products, it's quite similar to what I have written above. Manufacturing is all about continuous fine-tuning to make the optimized level of production. I remember Professor Kasra Ferdows teaching us in his MBA class about how business operations is about thinking about the big picture but also working on making the smallest details and perfecting the craft to make your production more effective. IoT-infused smart factories and smart cities can make this happen really easily. All you need is sensors implanted in every phase of the production and delivery phase that transmit data of the whereabouts of your product in real time and a command center that watches over everything in real time to decipher any problems that are foreseeable from the lucid operations that technology can bring.

This part will effectively talk about the potentials that this technology can bring to various sectors in business and why IoT will bring innovation and revamp the entire economy to its new efficient heights. This part will also talk about past instances of how IoT-like systems were in place in businesses that gave them such tremendous advantage over their competitors and also talk about the future potential if the businesses can hone these techniques. Also, this part will talk about the vulnerabilities that such connectivity will bring to our security systems and what needs to be focused on to make sure that we do not do harm by embracing technology in our economy.

CONNECTIVITY AND MANUFACTURING

In the book called *Prediction Machines* by Ajay Agrawal, Joshua Gans, and Avi Goldfarb, it talks about how data will be utilized for the betterment that brings not only value to the customers that are using it but to society in general. Digital connectivity happens in all forms. 5G is very important, but how content is created from the advanced network that will enable changes in life must involve data. What the book *Prediction Machines* and Hosuk Lee-Makiyama, a Brussels-based economist and trade lawyer and foreign policy commentator, said in an event at Brookings Institute was that "Data is the new oil of the twenty-first century." Meaning that whoever has control of it will determine the way companies make profits and state entities make policies.

The role of data for digital connectivity is critical. It is the meat of the content that will be streaming from a person's device to the servers of companies that will be existing online with 5G that will turn bundles of data into discernible intelligence for decision-making. One example that the book *Prediction Machines* has provided was a start-up called Cardiogram. This start-up is offered through an iPhone app that uses "heart rate data from an Apple Watch to generate an extraordinary amount of information: a second-by-second measure of heart rates for everyone who uses the app. Users can see when and if their heart rates spike over the course of a day and whether their heart rates have sped up or slowed down over a year or even a decade."(page 44, *Prediction Machines*) All this really means is that this app needs two things to collect a massive amount of data about people's heart rates to make predictions about heart attacks:

1. The device with sensors that enable such tracking to happen.
2. Connectivity that can transmit this data real time from doctor to patient. The technology for tracking is available with a plethora of devices out there in the market.

Already, we have brands like the Apple Watch and Fitbit that enable people to create such devices for measurements. And with advanced networks that are going to happen in the future, like 5G, I am confident that there can be devices that enable people to monitor their vitals and their life cycles better to boost longevity and productivity by enabling tremendous amount of data to flow through from the customer to the service providers that will enable better decision-making and product management.

So, what else can this device do to enhance productivity? From the operations class I took with Professor Ferdows, companies like Boeing are trying to incorporate IoT devices into their production line and their finished products so that when the product (engines for commercial airliners) is out in the market, it collects data of its usage and streamlines it back to Boeing.

Then, Boeing can get real-time information about the engine that is being used by different businesses and can analyze the type of problems or upgrades that occur which can be used to make sure that the next version of their jet engines can have newly updated features from these live feedbacks. The data collected from the engines will be incorporated in their planning phase, and the IoT devices in each of the production machines will also acknowledge the changes in design or any components that will make the product better and automatically adjust their production line to effectively suit the production of the new engines.

These methods of getting data as means of direct feedback from the products that are already operating in the field are highly effective for analyzing room for improvement for companies that offer them.

In my conversation with many staff members from many different smartphone manufacturers (who I cannot disclose due to their request), many of the smartphones also gather customer preference data and the errors they had when they were using the devices. The companies use the data gathered and make sure that their next generation's lineup do not have these kinds of problems. This will enable a faster rate of product improvements and can spur an earlier release of existing products that are more effective than their predecessors.

Many automobile companies are trying to harness such automation in processes in their manufacturing from input to output and incorporating it with the data they have received from their customers using their vehicles for everyday use. These intelligent automation systems will allow manufacturing companies to be able to harness large amounts of data to use as a form of intelligence to make predictions of where the product needs improving and the new set of items and improvements that must be incorporated when developing new models.

For example, General Motors and Toyota are developing this system by having a joint venture known as New United Motor Manufacturing, Inc. (NUMMI). "GM CEO Roger Smith pitched the idea that GM would gain some technology and insights into Toyota's production system, and Toyota would get a taste of trying to apply its systems and culture on a US workforce."[54]

Tech-savvy car companies like Tesla have already been infusing IoT and AI technology in their operations to better enhance their vehicles. Also, "Carmakers in the United States have reached an agreement with Department of Transportation to make automatic emergency braking standard on vehicles by 2022"[55]. If you go to Tesla Motors Club online, there is an article written by member "jmdavis" on December 12, 2016, that his Tesla saved his life through automatic emergency braking that avoided hitting the car in front of him.[56]

"The sensors embedded in the user's car not only enable vehicles to predict danger up ahead through programs that enable the activation when the distance and the movement of any

54 "Automating Intelligently Is Tesla's Manufacturing Advantage." CleanTechnica, June 26, 2018.

55 Agrawal, Ajay, Joshua Gans, and Avi Goldfarb. Prediction Machines: the Simple Economics of Artificial Intelligence. Boston, MA: Harvard Business Review Press, 2018.

56 Agrawal, Ajay, Joshua Gans, and Avi Goldfarb. Prediction Machines: the Simple Economics of Artificial Intelligence. Boston, MA: Harvard Business Review Press, 2018.

objects show aberrations in their movements, but they also send data related to the accidents and road conditions to Tesla HQ, where the company uses the massive amounts of data gathered from these sensors to create a predictive algorithm for all vehicles to better serve their customers' safety." (page 111, Prediction Machines)[57]

The predictive system that is used in manufacturing (which will be explained more later on) require an immense amount of data that cannot be fathomed for AIs and machines to predict and create needed judgement for organizations to take that will enable a better return in the future. Such data gathering must be done by devices that are in the forefront of the user experience.

The sensors that are incorporated in our smart devices all serve that purpose. It's no longer a world where companies must send out emails of surveys to get customer feedback. The usage of their product is enough to make sure that their feedback is heard. There may be issues with privacy of the users that are using it, and this is something that government and businesses should get together and talk about before 5G is launched that will enable this kind of data gathering and prediction machines to take place. Privacy is another issue

57   Agrawal, Ajay, Joshua Gans, and Avi Goldfarb. Prediction Machines: the Simple Economics of Artificial Intelligence. Boston, MA: Harvard Business Review Press, 2018.

that needs to be dealt with, but the notion that customer service and product improvement can happen at a unbelievably fast pace from incorporating IoT sensor technology into modern day products. These applications can be found most in how manufacturing adapts this to provide flexible products for customers all over the internet.

INTRODUCTION OF SMART MANUFACTURING

The Internet of Things is expected to have an impact in every facet of business today. And as explained, manufacturing is no exception. McKinsey estimates that the economic impact of the Internet of Things in factories by 2025 has the potential to grow to $3.7 trillion per year. Also, IBM Think Academy predicts that global productivity can increase by 25 percent with the use of Internet of Things in their manufacturing lines.[58] Internet of Things and advancement of manufacturing is the intersection between operational technology and information technology to monitor physical process within manufacturing and use data to make accurate and predictive decisions to improve operational cost and increase output for enhanced revenue generating opportunity.[59]

---

58 Academy, IBM Think. "How It Works: The Internet of Things and Manufacturing." YouTube. YouTube, November 10, 2016.

59 Anixter. "What Is Industry 4.0 and Smart Manufacturing?" YouTube. YouTube, May 9, 2018.

FROM HIGH TECHNOLOGY REQUIREMENT
TO HIGH FLEXIBILITY REQUIREMENT

Such affordable ways of manufacturing leave companies more able to be flexible with their production than they were when the new iPhone was first being developed. I have had semiconductor companies ask for more flexibility in our company's capacity because of high demand fluctuations; hence, manufacturing companies now must focus on operating in a world where changes are frequent, and only the ones with smooth operations will gain market share. Five years ago, manufacturing firms usually had flagship products, where the majority of their product lines were designated for a single or few products. Now companies are in high demand for a flexible operating line, and we have to make sure that our manufacturing operations reflect such characteristics of market fluctuations in demand.

This move toward smart manufacturing is defined by the National Institute of Standards and Technology as "fully-integrated, collaborative manufacturing systems that respond in real time to meet changes, demands, and conditions in the factory, in the supply network, and in customer needs." This also means that there should be a vertical and horizontal digital integration across all aspect of business.[60]

---

60 Anixter. "What Is Industry 4.0 and Smart Manufacturing?" You-Tube. YouTube, May 9, 2018.

An example of a vertical integration is a digital connection that goes from procurement, manufacturing, supply chain, design, product management, and logistics to sales, all integrated seamlessly in one system. A horizontal digitization will mean an integration of data within suppliers and key partners. Achieving this will require upgrading or replacing equipment networks and processes to create a digital ecosystem. Of course, however, integration itself will not bring any benefit to businesses without analytics and intelligence to decipher data into meaningful knowledge for business operations.

PAST INSTANCES OF USING DATA FOR OPERATIONAL EFFICIENCY

When I was taking my operations class in Georgetown University, I saw a quote from the legendary former CEO of Seven-Eleven Japan, Toshifumi Suzuki, who said, "Data without intelligence is dangerous." The best example of a vertically and horizontally integrated digital integration can be seen in companies like Seven-Eleven Japan, the largest and most profitable retail chain store in Japan, which has embraced the use of information systems in their supply chain management systems since the 1970s.

An article published by Stanford School of Business that can be read in the *Harvard Business Review* makes it clear how this company uses information to target their operations efficiency to the hilt to make sure that their 12,000-foot convenience stores are run with the lowest possible inventory while meeting customer demand. They use an information collection and feedback loop to make sure that all integration happens with their manufacturers and with their supplier as well. Their point of sales (POS) system has revolutionized management of stock keeping units (SKUs). The two-way communication between supply chains and manufacturers makes enabled franchises able to directly access the central database containing the POS data and analysis.[61]

To help with the definition below, "SC system" stands for Store Computer and "GOT" stands for Graphic Order Terminal.[62]

61 Whang, Seungjin, Hide Saito, Steve Van Horne, Casey Koshijima, and Takafumi Ueda. "SEVEN-ELEVEN JAPAN." Stanford: STANFORD GRADUATE SCHOOL OF BUSINESS, May 23, 2006.

62 Whang, Seungjin, Hide Saito, Steve Van Horne, Casey Koshijima, and Takafumi Ueda. "SEVEN-ELEVEN JAPAN." Stanford: STANFORD GRADUATE SCHOOL OF BUSINESS, May 23, 2006

Information Collection and Feedback Loop

Information about product sales captured at the register is passed on to SEJ's HQ via the fiber-optic network. In addition, the clerk keys in the customer's gender and estimated age on a separate keypad to supplement sales data. On average, 1,019 customers go to each store every day, resulting in more than 13 million customer data points per day. The POS data collected at each store is processed by the SC system. The SC enables the store manager and SEJ's HQ to update and analyze POS data simultaneously. Store managers can obtain real-time information through the GOT on site, thus allowing the manager to analyze the following data:

- *Hourly sales trend for individual items.* This information can be reviewed hourly, daily, or weekly, allowing the manager to optimize delivery schedules and minimize scrap levels. For example, suppose that the POS data showed that 10 cheese sandwiches delivered at 7:00 a.m. were sold out by 10:00 a.m. Because the next delivery truck would not arrive until noon, the store would lose all potential cheese sandwich sales until noon. The store manager could, however, choose to increase the future order quantity delivered at 7:00 a.m. to avoid a similar situation the next day. Another example involves a more sophisticated analysis of customer sales data. The POS data show that plum onigiri (rice balls) began to sell only after tuna onigiri delivered at the same time were sold out. From this information, the store manager could see that plum onigiri were being sold as a substitute for tuna onigiri. Next time, the store manager might increase the order quantity of tuna onigiri and decrease that of plum onigiri.
- *Scrap trend analysis.* Scrap trend analysis of individual items is important not just because of the associated scrap costs, but also because of the opportunity cost of the shelf space. By monitoring how long each item stays on the shelf, the store manager can better stock the store with fast-moving products.
- *Stockout ranking by individual items.* This information is especially important to manage fast food items that require freshness and timely delivery.
- *Sales trends for new products.* This information builds the basis for decisions in merchandising and new product development.
- *Hourly sales trends by customer profile.* This information is most useful to manufacturers for marketing purposes and is passed upstream for analysis.

As seen above, the information collection and the intelligence that is incorporated within SEJ makes them phenomenally efficient in inventory management. Also, "Such management and analytics of data can help segment customers by region to better predict what their needs are so that they can strategically deliver goods per weather and environmental conditions to make sure that their operations can mitigate the risk of stock shortages while not incurring unnecessary inventory costs."[63]

Location/Trade Area Analysis

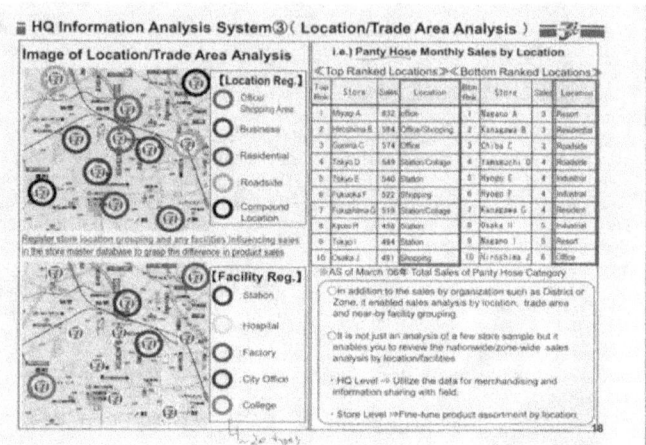

As you can see above, SEJ has had a location/trade area analysis over different regions and places and has made sure which items have priority over the others so that fast inventory management can happen to make sure they can optimize their business profits. This makes SEJ have the highest average sales per store per day among leading convenience store chains.

63 Whang, Seungjin, Hide Saito, Steve Van Horne, Casey Koshijima, and Takafumi Ueda. "SEVEN-ELEVEN JAPAN." Stanford: STANFORD GRADUATE SCHOOL OF BUSINESS, May 23, 2006

THE NEED FOR SMART MANUFACTURING

I would like to elaborate more on what I wrote about KT (Korea Telecom) and their advertisements about 5G and IoT. I have written earlier that 5G will bring new grounds for digital transformations for businesses. That can be said more about manufacturing than any other aspect of business. If you go to a blog managed by KT, they elaborate more on how the effects of IoT can foster greater efficiency in the workforce when robotics that are embedded with sensors are working with humans in the working plant, while advanced connectivity like 5G will enable a collaboration between humans and machine to be faster.[64]

According to the KT—this was written in Korean, so I am translating and at the same summarizing their blog—the 5G era will have the highest impact on manufacturing where the new concept of smart manufacturing is when IoT, big data (mass data), cloud computing, and manufacturing are infused together and powered by the next-generation connectivity known as 5G. It's an industry that will enable a new level of cooperation between humans and machines. This will make manufacturing more efficient, which will lead to practices that are more ecofriendly from being efficient with the materials used and, above all, be omni connected (this is a term I created). There is more information to be found

---

64 Yoohooo. "세상 모든 새로움의 시작, KT 5G 스마트 팩토리." 늘 곁에 kt, KT그룹 블로그. TISTORY, February 12, 2019.

in their blog, which is https://blog.kt.com/1282. I believe this can create a new range of efficiency in the manufacturing world that can make higher-spec industrial or consumer goods at a lower cost.

The above picture taken from KT's blog explains how the machines in the manufacturing line can work with humans by identifying the movements of their human counterparts to assist with fine processes in manufacturing or with heavy lifting. Also, the data can be stored and shared with other robots in the manufacturing line (through sensors or radio-wave receivers) to make sure that same kind of work can be performed in other parts of the production phase as well. This can exponentially decrease the learning cost that can be a key factor in production yield management and quality control.

Lowering learning cost is important because think of all the on-the-job training you have received to be proficient at something you worked on. Human beings take a lot of time to master a craft or a skillset. For basic mundane and high-labor required work, we can do this easily though transferring learned data through each machine. This can decease the time we need to train employees. Basically, infusing IoT technology can change the way humans and robotics work together as well. Humans can be more productive by focusing on high-value judgment and communications when robotics infused with sensor technology can assist humans on repetitive, labor-intensive tasks.

The above picture taken from KT's blog explains the power of sensor technology embedded in trucks to monitor their logistics in real time with autonomous driving that will enable faster delivery and also enable data to be shared through the supply chain to make accurate estimates on time of arrival to control manufacturing products more efficiently.

THE DANGER OF TECHNOLOGY IN AN INTANGIBLE MARKET

From my past experiences in component manufacturing and discussions I had in sessions and classes I took at Georgetown University, most of the developed countries are aware of this change and are racing to get the piece of the smart devices incorporated in the manufacturing. Financial markets are great for seeing short-term growth, but we have seen financial crisis in the world where wealth can be wiped out in minutes for millions of people. I was living in Seoul when the Asian Financial Crisis hit Korea in the 1990s. The amount of wealth that was wiped out from the South Korean market was devastating enough to ruin families financially.

I saw this happen again during 2008, when I was finishing up college at Indiana University, and I witnessed the effect of another financial crisis. I began to realize that wealth that was built on betting on values of intangible securities will have traumatic effects because wealth, like all things in life, is "easy come and easy go," and depending on how easy it is, it's that much easier to lose it. It's that one bad day in the market that will create losses so huge that it could tumble value into the negative. Developed countries are in love with financial markets. Most of my friends in business school opt to be financial experts after earning their MBA, and I can see why: this can seem so lucrative to the human eye. This short-term fantasy of financial snowballing is attractive to the human mind because of the money it generates in the short term. But there must be an understanding that this activity, of just trading derivatives or securities online, does not derive nor create meaningful and tangible sustainable value to the general public. The average person earns value from the money he earns when he purchases tangible goods with the salary he or she earns.

I love studying business, it is my joy to learn about the new growing markets and find out how they are benefiting our lives, which is why I decided to write this book in the first place. Business is supposed to make people's lives better by making the general public more fruitful. It is not something that is supposed to inflate prices for the sake of appreciating (increasing) something off of a "calculated" speculation. When finance is absent of the idea and the value it was supposed to finance, and it only focuses on the very few people that trade commodities or derivatives, will not only diminish opportunity for value creation for the average worker but also put the entire system at risk for a bubble burst that is caused by sheer speculation. However, with a firm root in manufacturing or businesses that are out to create value to the everyday customers around the world, its tangible value will be less likely to make the economy vulnerable to financial crisis that could hit the market with a storm and leave everyone penniless. Especially with the introduction of algorithms in the financial markets, we are seeing more turbulence in the financial markets. The Motley Fool has explained the dangers of algorithms in stock market the best:

"One major disadvantage of algorithmic trading is that one simple mistake can rapidly escalate in a major way. It's one thing for a trader to make a bad call and lose money on a single transaction, but when you have a faulty algorithm, the results can be downright catastrophic. That's because a single algorithm can trigger hundreds of transactions in a matter of minutes, and if something goes wrong, millions of dollars can be lost in that same time frame.

In fact, there have been multiple incidents of 'flash crashes' on global markets resulting from problems with algorithmic trading. For example, algorithmic trading was blamed for the 'Flash Crash' of 2010, which led US stock indexes to collapse (though they rebounded within an hour), as well as an October 2016 crash that saw the British pound plunge toward its thirty-one-year-low in a single night.

Algorithmic trading has also been linked to significant market volatility. While quality control measures can help prevent losses owing to poorly defined or coded algorithms, investors should be aware of the dangers of giving up control and letting computers do all of the work."[65]

There are aspects of business where computers or AIs can thrive in. Machines can populate data faster and can multi-task mundane rudimentary tasks a lot faster than the average human mind (as I have said before). Hence, such problems can arise if these machines are free to roam the digital trading world. However, in manufacturing, there can be an opportunities where machines and humans can coincide to create better value.

PRIVATE AND PUBLIC SECTORS

Much like the examples given above, Germany, the US, Japan, and many developed countries are trying to spearhead into this market. However, such movement in manufacturing development through IoT devices will not be possible without government subsidies. For example, education, training, and connecting the manufacturing workforce requires an in-depth collaboration between the state and the private sector. The manufacturing sector is facing wide gaps between emerging jobs and workers with needed skills. Traditional educational and technical skills are no longer enough.

---

65 Staff, Motley Fool. "What Is Algorithmic Trading?" The Motley Fool. The Motley Fool, April 27, 2017.

According to the Advanced Manufacturing Strategic Plan 2018,

"New technological literacies and cognitive capacities such as data competence and systems thinking will be needed for the work of tomorrow. To prepare the STEM (Science, Technology, Engineering, Math) workforce for future manufacturing jobs, national investments should prioritize lifelong STEM education—across elementary, high school, career and technical education (CTE), community colleges, universities, academic laboratories—and include diversified platforms for hands-on learning and self-directed learning. Other priorities for investment include apprenticeships, internships, traineeships, and other applied earn-and-learn models." [66]

"If there can be an effective way for government support to take place to educate the workforce to be able to adapt to the workforce that is consisting of IoT devices, productivity will increase where jobs will be created that adds value to the economy that can sustain the next industrial revolution. Advanced manufacturing plays an important role in agricultural production, food processing, and food safety. The safety of the food supply is vitally important, and improved food manufacturing practices

---

66 "STRATEGY FOR AMERICAN LEADERSHIP IN ADVANCED MANUFACTURING." *STRATEGY FOR AMERICAN LEADERSHIP IN ADVANCED MANUFACTURING*, SUBCOMMITTEE ON ADVANCED MANUFACTURING COMMITTEE ON TECHNOLOGY, Oct. 2018,

are needed to reduce uncertainty, improve inspection, and instill traceability into the supply chain."[67]

The demand for organic food is increasing in the US. As you can see in the graph below by Statista, there is a constant increase in demand for this sector in agriculture.[68]

Organic food sales in the United States from 2005 to 2017 (in billion U.S. dollars)

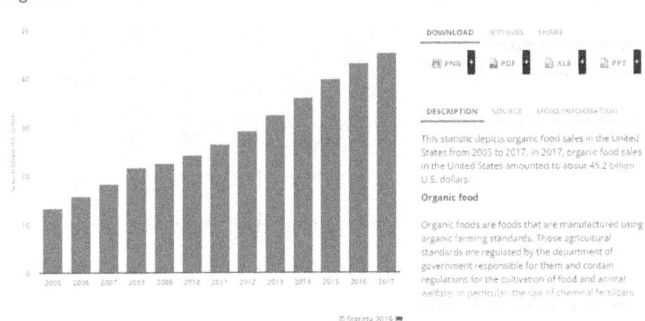

With more people becoming aware of the need for organic food, improved food manufacturing will enable customers to order food and can backtrack the specific dates and processes that the food they ordered has been through before it reaches their refrigerator. For example, when you order eggs (or any food with high sensitivity for freshness) from

67 "STRATEGY FOR AMERICAN LEADERSHIP IN ADVANCED MANUFACTURING." *STRATEGY FOR AMERICAN LEADERSHIP IN ADVANCED MANUFACTURING*, SUBCOMMITTEE ON ADVANCED MANUFACTURING COMMITTEE ON TECHNOLOGY, Oct. 2018,

68 "Organic Food Sales in the U.S. 2017 | Statista." Statista. Accessed May 30, 2019.

an online grocery store like Amazon.com, the buyer will be able to discover with a click of the button not only where the egg is from but also which supply chain was responsible for the delivery of the product. This can also enable more transparency in the supply chain of agricultural products, which can improve cost savings and the awareness of stricter quality control.

There are many strings of supply chains in the agricultural industry that no one really knows for sure; for example, when you buy your fruit from a local mart, it's not easy to find where this fruit was from and how it was carried. Unless it's a snack bar that has been regulated to disclose its nutrition information on the back of the bar, no food item in the world reveals how your food was delivered, which in my opinion is as important as what it is made of. If there can be a way to provide more transparency for the users, then there can surely be a way for companies to lean out their supply chains and, at the same time, have consumers be more assured that what they are receiving is a trustworthy product.

IT'S MANUFACTURING THAT BRINGS VALUE

On March 15, 2019, Tesla was unveiling the new Model Y. I was listening in on Elon Musk, the founder of Tesla, presenting to the public on their new model on YouTube[69]. During Mr. Musk's speech, I couldn't help but be impressed by what he said about manufacturing. He said, "Products, but then the factories, are as much a part (if not more) than the vehicles themselves. In fact, I really think like the difficulty and value of manufacturing is underappreciated; it's insanely difficult." It's true. I have been working for a hardware manufacturer, and like Mr. Musk said, "mass manufacturing products reliably and at scale" is something that requires dedication and time and effort, which is a culmination of craftsmanship and engineering. Also, I believe that it's mass manufacturing, whether cars or agricultural goods, that brings value to the largest number of lives.

When integrating advanced software with an intangible market like the financial markets, the trading volume and speed increase will only cause more mayhem from the volatility it brings. However, if machines are helping people with more tangible work, that is visible and has to obey the law of physics like every other human being, then there can be a potential for sustainable growth.

The manufacturing index is proof that the manufacturing sector is not as interesting or exciting as the financial world, but it is manufacturing that creates jobs. It's manufacturing

---

69   Tesla. "Model Y Unveil." YouTube. YouTube, March 15, 2019.

that creates value, and it was manufacturing that always fostered the bubble-less industrial revolution that created sustainable value for generations. It's time the internet and connectivity had a hand in the next industrial revolution, and most developed countries are aware that interconnectivity between devices and advanced software (AI) and big-data analytics can be a way to bring this to fruition.

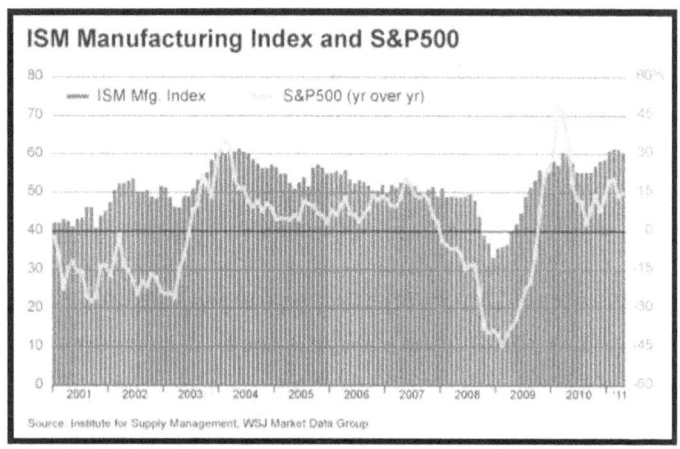

If you look at the chart above, despite the fact that manufacturing is not the main driver in the US economy, the ISM (Institute for Supply Management) manufacturing index explains that the manufacturing industry plays a significant role in the economy. The manufacturing industry made up of "13 percent of the GDP at the end of 2009, according to University of Michigan professor Mark Perry. The close relationship between ISM and GDP seems odd at first, but it might not be that odd. Manufacturing is still highly sensitive to shifts in the pace of global growth, and the S&P 500 is dominated by companies that export goods around the world."[70]

Also, from the chart we can conclude that the manufacturing index is less sensitive to financial crisis when you look at 2008. When banks and insurance companies were filing for bankruptcy, the manufacturing index's drop seems to be less sensitive than other industries in the S&P 500. Even though the auto industry received a bailout package, it seems that the wheels were continuously churning in factories. This proves that manufacturing is a sector that drives sustainability and healthy growth. This is certainly a sector that needs to be revamped, and information technology and connectivity are surly seen as viable options to make manufacturing lean and profitable again without having to outsource everything overseas.

America, on the other hand, is creating a consortium of companies called the Smart Manufacturing Leadership Coalition that can create a synergy effect for the Internet of Things market. Such synergies are expected to come from a wide variety of different tech sectors such as big data analysis, AI, and robotics. Also, the American government has created the Advanced Manufacturing National Program Office

---

70 Gongloff, Mark. "ISMs Svengali-Like Hold on the Stock Market." The Wall Street Journal. Dow Jones & Company, May 31, 2011.

(AMNPO) to further enhance the manufacturing innovation networks with cutting-edge interconnectivity.

"Hosted by the Department of Commerce at the National Institute of Standards and Technology (NIST), the AMNPO is an interagency team with participation from federal agencies involved in advanced manufacturing. Principal participant agencies currently include the Departments of Commerce, Defense, Education, and Energy, the National Aeronautics and Space Administration, and the National Science Foundation. Established in 2012, the AMNPO reports to the Executive Office of the President and operates under the NSTC (National Science and Technology Council) on cross-agency initiatives. The office reports to the Secretary of Commerce in its role as the 'the National Office of the Network for Manufacturing Innovation Program,' also referred to as the 'National Program Office,' as described by the Revitalize American Manufacturing and Innovation Act of 2014."[71]

Manufacturing priorities are equally important for food and nonfood applications, such as advances in seed production from the mathematical optimization of plant breeding, improving plant productivity and resilience, lowering costs of processing and conversion, ensuring worker safety, and improving efficiencies throughout the supply

---

71 "The Advanced Manufacturing National Program Office." Manufacturing.gov. Accessed May 30, 2019.

chain. Advanced processing and supply chain integration are needed to improve the functionality and lower the cost of bio-based products.[72]

New ways of producing have a lot to do with providing the adequate flexibility for production to bring customer satisfaction. Such flexibility has a lot to do with making sure that manufacturers are comfortable with changes that can bring a halt to their production line in the middle of high-volume manufacturing or at the end design phase of the production. To elaborate more on the subject, I will share a personal experience I had when I was an account manager at a component manufacturer.

In June 2017, I was an account manager for a manufacturing company that made circuit boards, and I was exposed to products that required being part of a complex supply chain that reached across many different countries all over the world. Products like smart glasses (depicted is below), which were a new product and had a complex supply chain because it involved a mix of both conventional glassmakers and state-of-the-art semiconductor manufacturers.

---

72 "The Advanced Manufacturing National Program Office." Manufacturing.gov. Accessed May 30, 2019.

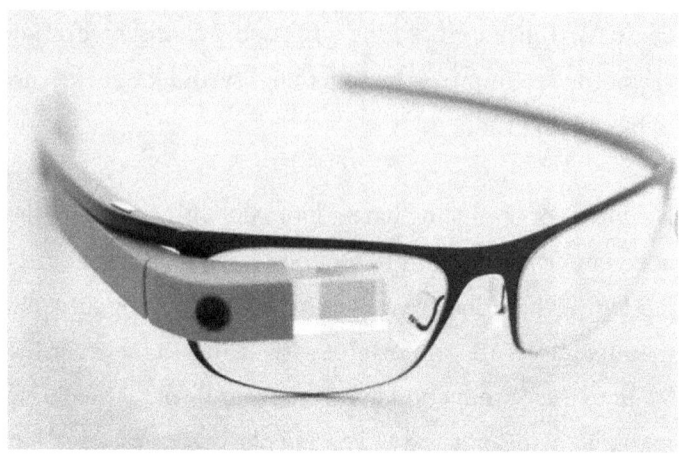

The picture above is a smart glass made by Google; it was discontinued in 2015.[73]

The first thing we needed to do after we signed the account was to receive the design for the product that we were going to make. Circuit boards were basically like the bone structure of the product; hence, design and power requirements were of the essence, and the delivery also had to be made on time since it was one of the first components used in assembly. The design was something totally new since glasses had two sides (obviously, because we have two eyes), which comprised of the left side being the battery and the right side being the part that does all the work, such as allowing athletes to monitor their heart rate and speed of their movement, etc.

73 Getty. "Amazon Is Working on a Pair of Google Glass-Style Smart Glasses Powered by Alexa." mirror, September 20, 2017.

Once we negotiated the price and the delivery time of the product, we received a go sign to start our samples for testing. The lead time (manufacturing time) needed for the product was faster than our usual circuit boards for smart phones or smart watches since it involved a lot of players in the supply chain, so we had to move fast, and we had to procure raw materials and make sure that our manufacturing lines could make swift adjustments whenever there was a design change faster than any other IT products we had ever worked on.

FLEXIBILITY TO ITS CORE

Given the fact that IoT devices demand high cross-product compatibility, the design changes happen frequently because the requirements can change depending on how the end customer will be using the product. IoT devices are sensitive to changes in content, meaning that if the end customer is using content in a different way, then it is natural the design of the devices should also change to maximize value for the user. This requires adaptations to fast changes in manufacturing and also various supply chains.

As Jeff Bezos, the founder of Amazon.com, said,

"When thinking through an IoT solution, what is most obvious is the end device. But this is the classic 'tip of the iceberg' in creating end-to-end solutions. The IoT Value Chain is defined

by devices, connectivity, big data, algorithms, actions, and connection to the rest of the enterprise. As more and more IoT devices get introduced, a greater amount of data (both big and small) is generated. This data, once integrated with algorithms, create a greater overall customer IoT impact generating more demand for more devices. All of these devices and services can be hosted on Amazon Web Services (AWS) and utilize their infrastructure capabilities, leading to greater growth of the infrastructure."

"At this point, the loop looks familiar: infrastructure growth leads to lower costs, which means more services and companies rely on the infrastructure locking into a cycle of higher customer impact. Amazon Web Services has several existing IoT-enabling products including AWS Redshift, AWS Kinesis, AWS Machine Learning, and the acquisition of 2lemetry shows that the big bet for Amazon is not in creating devices for its retail business, but in providing cloud infrastructure and software to thousands of companies needing to build IoT devices and capabilities. This is the AWS IoT flywheel and the real business in IoT for Amazon."[74]

This means that the bullwhip effect of that is felt on the supply chain more since there is greater need for changes needed

---

74 Mythemes. "Jeff Bezos | Stephenson Blogs on Internet of Things - Internet of Things Strategy, Breakthroughs and Management." Stephenson blogs on Internet of Things. Accessed May 30, 2019.

per the data and the infrastructure growth from the content that will create and change ways devices are used. Satya Nadella, the CEO of Microsoft, agrees with this characteristic of the IoT devices market; in an interview with *The Inquirer*, Nadella said,

"Digital technology, pervasively, is getting embedded in every place: everything, every person, every walk of life is being fundamentally shaped by digital technology—it is happening in our homes, our work, our places of entertainment. It's amazing to think of a world as a computer. I think that's the right metaphor for us as we go forward."[75]

SO, HOW WILL THIS IMPACT OUR FUTURE LIKE THE BOOK SAYS IN 2030?

Data is becoming a more and more important part of analyzing and predicting the future. It's not an exaggeration to say that companies like Seven-Eleven Japan used a primitive version of what IoT will bring to our future by organizing user preferences by gathering data of users per different locations to make sure that their convenience stores will be equipped with necessary goods to make sure to capture the demand trends as accurately as possible. They did this by not only

---

75 "Microsoft's Satya Nadella Reckons the World's a Computer Thanks to AI and IoT Tech | TheINQUIRER." http://www.theinquirer.net, May 23, 2018.

gathering data but also by making sure that their orders' and shelves' replenishment were made seamlessly throughout Japan. (See below diagram for better illustration.)[76]

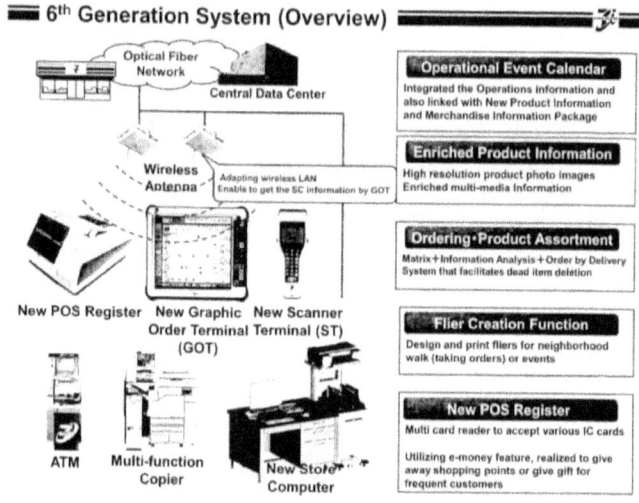

Now let's say we have affordable devices with sensors that can be attached to each shipment, and each store shelf and every single block in cities to help monitor the progress of the shipments, also the speed at which the products are being sold as well to make sure that the goods will be replenished on shelves without delays while helping the convenience store managers keep the lowest possible inventory (because if you have stacks of inventory, it eats up space and money and also,

76 Whang, Seungjin, Hide Saito, Steve Van Horne, Casey Koshiji-ma, and Takafumi Ueda. "SEVEN-ELEVEN JAPAN." Stanford: STANFORD GRADUATE SCHOOL OF BUSINESS, May 23, 2006

if its edible, freshness of the product). This will certainly be a future worth investing in and a future where people can look at logistics and retail differently with technology infused for more efficiency.

Seven-Eleven Japan was able to be the best retailer in Japan and outmaneuver their competitors because they knew how to gather data and convert data into information that could be used to minimize costs and deliver the correct amount of goods at the correct amount of need. Now let's say we can do this for the world, on a greater scale with better precision: a system that allows logistics and manufacturing to happen and deliver in real time across the world with close to zero margin of error.

For this to happen, we need infrastructure for roads and connectivity and accessibility of data not just for big corporations but also small to midsize firms that are making and delivering goods to people across the world. We need conventional manufacturing companies to embrace technologies and move away from the simple past of just making and delivering and processing orders. And most importantly, we need customers to be aware that there is technology out there that is available to us that can make our lives better and more convenient at a very low cost. We just need to know about the complex future and embrace the fact that we need to move away from the comfort of the simplicity that was our past.

FROM A SIMPLE PAST TO A COMPLEX FUTURE

For components like circuit boards, the business was simple back in the days when the average flip phone was the only means of transferring mobile data that was bringing customer value. Designs were fixed early in the production phase and supply chains usually moved in unison after the design was finalized. There were little changes within the production phase, and the certification for high volume runners took a very systematic process since having a concrete design and supply chain made it easy for companies within their supply chains to minimize uncertainties and also risks from having to face uncertainties in the future. For example, it would be terribly costly for a company like Samsung to change their design in midproduction after advertising its specs and design to the public.

When I was an account manager for a tablet PC maker, the design was set from the beginning, and pricing and capacity negotiations were based on the fixed design. If the customer wanted finer lining or expensive raw materials or a thinner product, then we made sure that the pricing and the capacity was adjusted for these higher needs.

If we experienced a technological advancement in our manufacturing, we made sure that the lead times and delivery schedules or production capacity was positively reflected in our future negotiations. All these changes integrated for business operations were possible because we were sure that the designs were fixed and that they were very unlikely to change.

This is not the case for IoT devices. The devices are small, highly compatible, and work on legacy technology, products that are older than the currently mass-manufactured generation. These devices have unexpected returns, and some devices even appear in the market only to see them wither and disappear within months. According to an article in Techinasia.com written by Malavika Velayanikal in 2016, most companies die within one year. Even in countries like

India, where tech start-ups are prevalent, there are many companies that fail to survive long-term.[77]

Hence, companies will be more likely to focus more on seeing how customers react to their products and try to make changes as fast as possible. Tech companies now need to be fast and agile like Zara, which is one of the leading fast fashion retailers that I will explain more about later, which focuses primarily on making sure that their new products are popular with customers and if they are not, they make sure that they can provide new products fast that can copy the popular ones and take the unpopular ones off the market as fast as possible. The operations for companies like Zara rely heavily on automated lines so any design changes or prototypes for mass production can be incorporated to their production line with the most immediate effect.

FAST FASHION AND PROOF OF NEED FOR NIMBLENESS

When it comes to operations and technology, Zara is one of the best companies in the world. There is a *Harvard Business Review* case article that explains their lean operations as below.

---

77 Tech in Asia - Connecting Asia's startup ecosystem. Accessed October 28, 2019

"Inditex (the parent company of Zara) is a pioneer among 'fast fashion' companies, which essentially imitate the latest fashions and speed their cheaper versions into stores. Every one of Inditex's brands—Zara, Zara Home, Bershka, Massimo Dutti, Oysho, Stradivarius, Pull & Bear, and Uterqü —follow the Zara template: trendy and decently made but inexpensive products sold in beautiful, high-end-looking stores. Zara's prices are similar to those of the Gap: coats for $200, sweaters for $70, T-shirts for $30."[78]

An article in *Harvard Business Review* called "Zara: The World's Largest Fashion Retailer" studies how efficient Zara is at operations with their usage of technology.

"Zara changes its clothing designs every two weeks on average, while competitors change their designs every two or three months. It carries about 11,000 distinct items per year in thousands of stores worldwide compared to competitors that carry 2,000 to 4,000 items per year in their stores. Zara's highly responsive supply chain is central to its business success. The heart of the company and its supply chain is a huge, highly automated distribution center (DC) called 'The Cube.'"

---

78   Hansen, Suzy. "How Zara Grew Into the World's Largest Fashion Retailer." *The New York Times*, The New York Times, 9 Nov. 2012,

The screenshot below shows a close-up satellite view of this facility.[79]

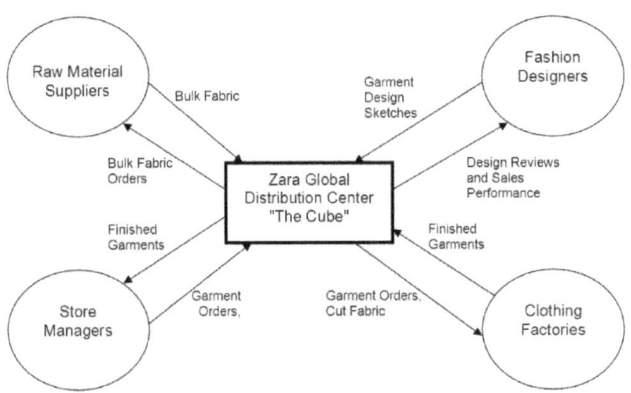

The picture requires an immense amount of fast changes and nimbleness in their manufacturing and supply chain. Also, since Zara produces most of their production in-house, their need for adaptability can happen better in-house.

"Factories can increase and decrease production quickly, thus there is less inventory in the supply chain and less need to finance that inventory with working capital. They do only 50–60 percent of their manufacturing in advance versus the 80–90 percent done by competitors. So, Zara does not need to place big bets on yearly fashion trends. They can make

79 Mhugos. "Zara Clothing Company Supply Chain." *SCM Globe*, 11 Mar. 2019,

many smaller bets on short-term trends that are easier to call correctly."[80]

Even if their production is easier to handle, their global demand has forced them to embrace technology to make sure their capacity will be flexible and nimble enough for fast production to take place. This means fully automating their production lines. Their need for CAPEX (or increase their current capacity for production) for better automation lines with a fully centralized system will make a vertical digitization with the company for seamless manufacturing.

To incorporate technology into efficient manufacturing, Zara had worked with some of the world's best suppliers and hardware and software to develop the system of these warehouse automations and had modified them by its own teams to fit its operations. For example, optical readers tracked the network of the overhead rails that connected the factories via underground tunnels to the distribution centers. Orders for each store were packed automatically in boxes from moving conveyors, and matched, and also automatically, with items on hangers for the same store in shipping areas.[81]

80 Mhugos. "Zara Clothing Company Supply Chain." *SCM Globe*, 11 Mar. 2019,

81 Ferdows, Kasra, Jose A.D. Machuca, and Michael A. Lewis. "Zara: The World's Largest Fashion Retailer." Wellesley: Case Centre, 2014.

THE ZARAS OF THE FUTURE: SMALLER
BUT MORE POWERFUL

When I was speaking with Professor Ferdows, my professor for operations at Georgetown University, he said that large companies invested heavily in maintaining a responsive manufacturing like Zara. However, they can do this because of the scale they provide and to make sure they have enough capacity to make sure that changes in their product design can happen within two weeks. "Zara, therefore, was quick to realize that there exists a direct relationship between the degree of capacity utilization of its factories and their length of turnaround times. In other words, the busier a factory, the longer it would take to manufacture a fast fashion item."[82]

However, with the advent of smart manufacturing, each piece of manufacturing equipment is embedded with these sensors that can make manufacturing super-efficient and fast. This can have an immense improvement in production capacity at a cheaper cost than what Zara had done as a huge multinational corporation. If sensor technology gets cheap enough, small to medium-sized companies can also have such production technology available for them to be agile and nimble to customer demand. By also having AIs analyzing data on their production system to suggest improvements, there can

---

82 "10 Trends in Digital Manufacturing Revealed in Latest Industrial IoT Survey Jointly Conducted by SME and Plataine." ManufacturingTomorrow. Accessed June 5, 2019.

be a new breed of lean manufacturing that can provide a cheaper way of producing their products.

A survey conducted by "SME, a manufacturing association promoting advanced manufacturing technologies" conducted a survey on how digitized manufacturing, in other words smart manufacturing is affecting our industries.[83]

SME's survey proved that IoT technology is being embraced by many established companies in that:

"Manufacturers from multiple industries including aerospace, automotive, furniture, and chemicals, were designed to help advanced manufacturing managers prepare for the rapid advances in digital technology that are transforming factories. The survey reveals how factories intend to implement new digital technologies, which challenges are faced, and what benefits they envision."

If these devices will mitigate the usage of paper-based processes, by having devices communicate with each to effectively control the utilization rate of each manufacturing phase and also foster collaboration between each player in the supply chain. These players, what I mean by manufacturers in supply

---

83   "10 Trends in Digital Manufacturing Revealed in Latest Industrial IoT Survey Jointly Conducted by SME and Plataine." ManufacturingTomorrow. Accessed June 5, 2019.

chain, will be able to effectively notify shortages in new products to ramp up production while slowing down production of those that are not in need and also robotics that can lend a hand that can do work that takes a lot of human capital.[84]

All this can enable smaller companies to act as fast and responsive as bigger companies or work with them in their supply chain easier without having any issues. When I was an account manager working with big tech manufacturers, the hardest part about being a component manufacturer in a huge supply chain is the cost of paperwork and aligning technical requirements. These costs not only eat up costs (money) but also take a lot of time and manpower even before actual manufacturing begins.

For example, there is a *Harvard Business Review* article about the supply chain collaboration between Lego and Flextronics didn't work because of these problems in collaboration and connectivity. Lego is one of the largest toy manufacturers in the world (no need for further explanation), and they tried to outsource their business to Flextronics to save costs. Flextronics was a "leading multinational electronics manufacturing service (EMS) provider based in Singapore,

---

84 "10 Trends in Digital Manufacturing Revealed in Latest Industrial IoT Survey Jointly Conducted by SME and Plataine." ManufacturingTomorrow. Accessed June 5, 2019.

had a long history of offering service to original equipment manufacturers (OEM)."[85]

Not only was Flextronics a larger company than Lego, but Flextronics does business with big companies such as Casio, Cisco Systems, Dell, Eastman Kodak, Ericsson, Hewlett-Packard, Microsoft, and Motorola. This was a classic example of a smaller company working with a behemoth to make their supply chain effective. Given Flextronics's specialty in manufacturing, it seemed like a good deal to outsource production. However, the marriage in supply chain did not go as planned.

"There was the challenge of aligning the Lego products' seasonal fluctuations and unpredictable demand with Flextronics's business model. About 60 percent of the Lego production was made in the second half of the year, the product had an average lifespan of sixteen to eighteen months, and the demand uncertainty fluctuated with plus or minus 30 percent. The Lego Group's need for flexible and market-responsive business solutions presented a strategic misfit with Flextronics's more stable and predictable operations in which economies of scale was a key phrase."[86]

85 Larsen, Marcus Moller, Toben Pedersen, and Dmitrij Slepniov. "LEGO GROUP: AN OUTSOURCING JOURNEY." Ontario: Ivey Publishing, 2010.
86 Larsen, Marcus Moller, Toben Pedersen, and Dmitrij Slepniov. "LEGO GROUP: AN OUTSOURCING JOURNEY." Ontario: Ivey Publishing, 2010.

The *Harvard Business Review* article also mentioned that system integration and also paperwork between the two companies were too burdensome. However, just imagine if those two companies were using sensors in their manufacturing plant and their procurement channels and had data flowing freely that could enable Lego to know exactly how the production was going and also enabling Flextronics to understand fluctuations in demand in real time from the data that flowed from each plant to shipments made to customers. The marriage between the two companies could have worked.

THE ADAPTIVE MINDSET

Such automation can happen on a larger scale as more companies adopt such an adaptive mindset toward customer needs. Imagine a world where this can happen faster with products such as cars that take a longer production phase and a lot more components to manufacture. Let's say, for example, a factory is running on a completely automated IoT system and the machines are incorporated with IoT devices, and the factory line operator is also wearing such devices as well. A sudden decision to change the design of the product or a potential malfunction in the product could be communicated to all the machines and operators in real time, and from such connectivity, information could be transmitted in an effortless but accurate way not only to operators on the manufacturing lines but also the machines too will know how to alter the designs or usage of raw materials. This would enable car manufacturers to come up with next-generation products faster.

This will mean that companies can no longer wait for the products to be perfect but need to adopt the lean manufacturing methods mentioned in Eric Ries's book *The Lean Startup*. Now, since the products need to be highly compatible to one another, design changes are prevalent. People will not use the devices if the content that was meant for a certain usage changes, like how car manufacturers like Tesla are going fully digital with their car systems that compel component manufactures to develop software and applications that are installed in their smartphones or any smart devices to start.

Such changes will force conventional manufacturers to make that leap and test their new products to see if their business plan works in the market; that people will use their applications on their phones to start their vehicle. Such products cannot wait until the product finishes its quality tests but need to adopt what Ries said that companies ought to do.

They should use a minimum viable product (MVP) that helps the business start the process of learning as quickly as possible. This can happen in the start, middle, or post development phase of the product, and businesses should be quick enough to make sure that the end customers can find the devices useful, or if the design needs changes, for delivering the best user experience in the quickest time possible.[87] This means companies need to be nimbler to design, make, and test their products, and then adapt to the customer's needs and wants almost instantly.[88]

LEGACY TECHNOLOGY AND SPEED

Thankfully, such pivoting and flexibility will be possible without having businesses live through the pain of creating something totally new. Whether it's creating wearable devices like health trackers or sensors that are implanted in your smart refrigerator to monitor the freshness of your produce, it is technology that has already been around. Connectivity can also be done cheaply as well. Ben Edwards works at a robotics company based in Boulder, Colorado, called Misty Robotics. Their mission is to put a personal robot in every home and office. Five years ago, the only robotics that were available for the world were in manufacturing; robotics was an expensive product, and it was highly unlikely they would be seen in households. However, technological advancement has allowed parts needed for home robotics to be more prevalent and less likely to be a showstopper than it was in the past.

---

87 Ries, Eric. Lean Startup. Place of publication not identified: Portfolio Penguin, 2017

88 Ries, Eric. Lean Startup. Place of publication not identified: Portfolio Penguin, 2017.

According to Edwards, such personalized robot technology will be available as an Internet of Things device for households within eight to ten years to open doors for working moms and working dads to share information via the personalized robotics at home. It could be available for affluent families at first, but like all technology goods, the cost of production decreases with time, and key components like sensors for object recommendation will be more available for most households.

Technology costs have always decreased with time. According to an article in *Business Insider*,

"Technological innovation is great for consumers. As technology gets more advanced, prices drop, and products get better. The US Bureau of Labor Statistics tracks prices for broad categories of goods over time. As this chart of prices for the last eighteen years shows, prices have dropped dramatically in almost every tech sector. The drop in computer hardware is particularly steep."[89]

---

89 Rosoff, Matt. "Every Type of Tech Product Has Gotten Cheaper over the Last Two Decades - except for One." Business Insider. Business Insider, October 14, 2015.

KEEPING FOOD FRESH FOR KIDS AT SCHOOL

IoT can also prevent food poisoning and make sure that your kids are eating fresh and healthy food when they are away at school or at daycare. I know a lot of friends and family members that have kids, and every day they have to leave their kids at school or at daycare (depending on their age, obviously). It would be the most unfortunate circumstance if you hear that your children were subject to food poisoning at a school cafeteria, and sometimes, with changing temperatures during summertime, it can be extremely difficult for teachers and nutritionists to monitor every ingredient down the supply chain to guarantee the freshness of the produce that is being used to feed millions of students every day.

JE Yeo, a former nutritionist who worked with the Ministry of Food and Drug Safety for public schools in Pohang, a city in South Korea, said that every public school in Pohang has implemented an early version of what is now being called IoT devices (sensor technology) in 2016 that enables all the inventories of fresh produce to be monitored. These sensors are placed in every refrigerator, buffet lines, and kitchens in public school cafeterias to monitor the temperature and humidity.

These sensors are connected into giant big-data center in the Ministry of Food and Drug Safety and also alert the teachers, nutritionists, supply chain experts, and local authorities when there is a foreseeable risk of food poisoning. Now, since these sensors were streaming data using 4G connectivity (according to Ms. Yeo every public schools in Pohang is fully connected with the latest 4G connections), there was a time lag of thirty minutes to an hour from the school cafeterias to the data centers. However, Ms. Yeo said that the time lag was sufficient enough to make preventive measures to avoid any major food poisoning from hurting millions of students that are eating lunch every day.

Like what is going on in the city of Pohang, IoT runs on multiple sensors that are implemented to monitor a certain situation and phenomenon. However, it takes connectivity from major infrastructure projects that ensure that these sensors will be able to move their monitored data to centers for analysis to alert the public of future dangers.

IT'S THE SENSOR TECHNOLOGY AND CONNECTIVITY

Hardware is not the problem, but the biggest problem is how to connect the hardware with software. Just imagine a working mom (let's call her Judy). She comes rushing home because her meeting has ended later than expected, and she needs to cook dinner for her two children before they go to their Taekwondo class. Now she needs to cook, clean, and drive to their afterschool activities.

This is not something that can be done all at once. There are certainly appliances available for all three activities to be done in a click of a button. Smart kitchen appliances and smart vacuum cleaners are sold by South Korean electronics companies. Although they care called smart kitchen appliances, they are not much smarter than a device that offers software on its own without any interconnectivity between multiple devices. It's funny how these products are called "smart-something," but the technology that these devices show today is only a single pairing technology that does not fully ascertain the full constructiveness that the IoT is supposed to bring. Hence, I think they are not smart yet. Samsung has been in the forefront of this technology and examples are made with their POWERbot automatic vacuum cleaning models.[90]

Samsung's POWERbot offers autocleaning and syncs to your phone, but it is still miles away from offering an autocleaning service via the need of the customer upon reacting to their activities.

Car manufacturers now have software for smartphones that enables cars to start through your smartphone, and navigation software that lets you know which route to take that

---

90 "SAMSUNG POWERbot™ ROBOT VACUUM." Samsung POWERbot™ Robot Vacuum | Special Offer, Features & Specs. Accessed June 5, 2019.

will get you there as fast as possible. However, that cannot happen all at once. The human brain just cannot handle that much multitasking after working a nine to five job nonstop, rushing home, and then cooking, cleaning, and watching over your children as they prepare to go out. It's hard, or at least for me, near impossible, to do it all at once (believe me, I tried and it's impossible to try it without making a mess of things). However, there is a platform where all the devices are connected.

Then those devices can truly act as IoT where the connectivity within each device mentioned above is linked together so that Judy can inform her smart kitchen devices to fire up her oven while she is driving into her home, have the smart vacuum/floor wiping cleaner start cleaning the kitchen floor and be ready to move on its own when there is a spill, and also if that connectivity can ensure that the car is started right as Judy leaves the apartment with her kids, it can immensely improve the future for all working moms who struggle to make time for their kids. Of course, technology for self-driving cars that can drive kids to their afterschool activities is another topic to discuss, but in terms of connectivity through sensors to detect motions and the software that can discern changes and procedures needed for their customer satisfaction, IoT devices will flourish and true digital connectivity can take place.

SMART MANUFACTURING CAN
BE A PRODUCT BY ITSELF

Part of the benefit of being a full-time MBA student at a respectable institution like Georgetown University McDonough School of Business is that you get exposed to a variety of business models and strategies that optimize business operations. One of my favorite classes was learning about the operations aspect of business. We are living in a time where 5G is about to bring a new platform for companies to take advantage of this connectivity and operate online. This will bring enormous opportunities for improvement in the way companies manage their manufacturing facilities to their optimal capacity.

Such connection will enable companies to infuse their manufacturing procedures with sensors and devices (IoT) that make sure that all phases of their manufacturing is done where line operators can be notified of expected bottlenecks by studying the flow of production via real-time sensors and machines that work in unison from input to output.

Imagine a factory line where line operators are not present unless there is a problem with sensors and manufacturing equipment. Entire control of the manufacturing line can be done automatically because the sensors enable devices to send the central control center (an operations center with a manufacturing staff present) to alert the level of utilization of the equipment and the flow of different products that is happening without having to check individual equipment and relying on floor managers in each phase to make sure that operations are running smoothly. In my operations class taught by Professor Ferdows, we learned about how companies like Boeing and Ikea are trying to implement the IoT in the manufacturing systems.

Microsoft, one of the leaders of developing IoT, is heavily investing in making sure they can take advantage of this opportunity. According to Julia White, who is the corporate vice president of Microsoft Azure, "Microsoft will invest $5 billion in the Internet of Things over the next four years. Our goal is to give every customer the ability to transform their businesses, and the world at large, with connected solutions."[91]

If you look at Microsoft's website, there are a variety of services that Microsoft is trying to provide to take the most advantage of the IoT technology. I won't talk too much about the services since all information is available online in the mentioned URL: https://azure.microsoft.com/en-us/overview/iot/industry/

---

91   "Azure IoT." Microsoft Azure. Accessed June 5, 2019

- **Monitor manufacturing equipment:** Improve your processes using industrial IoT solutions. Use sensors and advanced analytics to predict needed maintenance, and reduce unplanned downtime cutting into production time.
- **Provide predictive maintenance to customers:** Create new business models that offer predictive maintenance and performance monitoring for the equipment you produce, delivering a richer customer experience.
- **Improve field service:** Access sensor data to improve field service scheduling, ensuring the right technicians and tools are dispatched before potential issues become a major problem."

There are plenty of books published regarding smart manufacturing, and like Professor Ferdows said, there are many books and many articles published that talk about the fabulous benefits that the IoT will bring to manufacturing. However, there is no living data and proof of this technology being implemented in companies today. For example, just because Boeing announced that they are going to have a smart factory doesn't mean that it has it running 24/7 or that any of the new airlines have had a magnificent decrease in their costs because of such implementation of digital connectivity.

This remands me of early 2000s. Before Apple's iPhone was introduced and changed the way people transfer information at the touch of your fingers, there was a plethora of discussions going around in the tech industry about the concept of a smartphone.

I remember being in college back then and attending conferences and listening to guest speakers from tech speaking about how there could be a palm-sized device that could let people watch their favorite TV show on their phones and at the same time check their Facebook and chat with their friends. Such a story seemed like a far future for me when I was listening to it, and that the device could revolutionize the way of living. But this all changed after the release of the first iPhone. I still remember that speech given by Steve Jobs. Literally, the world was different after his speech on June 29, 2007.[92] As a person who is very interested in technology and the change that technology has in business and bringing value to the consumers, I am going to include the legendary speech that Steve Jobs gave when he introduced the first iPhone below.

"Every once in a while, a revolutionary product comes along that changes everything. And Apple has been—well, first of all, one's very fortunate if you get to work on just one of these in your career.

---

92 "iPhone." Wikipedia. Wikimedia Foundation, May 8, 2019.

Apple's been very fortunate. It's been able to introduce a few of these into the world. In 1984, we introduced the Macintosh. It didn't just change Apple, it changed the whole computer industry. In 2001, we introduced the first iPod, and...it didn't just—it didn't just change the way we all listen to music, it changed the entire music industry.

Well, today, we're introducing three revolutionary products of this class.

The first one: is a widescreen iPod with touch controls.

The second: is a revolutionary mobile phone.

And the third is a breakthrough internet communications device.

So, three things: a widescreen iPod with touch controls; a revolutionary mobile phone; and a breakthrough internet communications device.

An iPod, a phone, and an internet communicator. An iPod, a phone...Are you getting it? These are not three separate devices, this is one device, and we are calling it iPhone.

Today, today Apple is going to reinvent the phone, and here it is.

No, actually here it is, but we're gonna leave it there for now.

So, before we get into it, let me uh talk about a category of things. The most advanced phones are called smartphones. So they say.

And uh they typically combine a phone plus some email capability,

plus they say it's the internet.

It's sort of the baby internet, into one device,

and they all have these plastic little keyboards on them.

And the problem is that they're not so smart and they're not so easy to use, so if you kinda make a... Business School 101 graph of the smart axis and the easy-to-use axis, phones, regular cell phones are kinda right there, they're not so smart, and they're—you know—not so easy to use.

Umm...But smart phones are definitely a little smarter,

but they actually are harder to use. They're really complicated. Just for the basic stuff, a hard time figuring out how to use them.

Well, we don't wanna do either one of these things.

What we wanna do is make a leapfrog product that is way smarter than any mobile device has ever been, and super easy to use.

This is what iPhone is. OK?

So, we're gonna reinvent the phone."[93]

If 3G was built for consumer connectivity with the introduction of the iPhone, 5G is built for an industrial revolution (as mentioned in my previous chapter about 5G); this means that a smart factory could be the new iPhone.

Succeeding in building a smart factory will mean that the company can not only produce their products better but also can sell the concept of a smart factory as an item. We have companies that have a competitive edge in manufacturing sell their technology as a form of consulting to other manufacturing companies. Some of the greatest companies that we know today outsource their manufacturing to original equipment manufacturers (OEMs).

According to Wikipedia, "An original equipment manufacturer (OEM) is a company that produces parts and equipment that may be marketed by another manufacturer. For

---

93 Wright, Mic. "The Original iPhone Announcement Annotated: Steve Jobs' Genius Meets Genius." The Next Web, June 12, 2018.

example, Foxconn, a Taiwanese electronics contract manufacturing company, which produces a variety of parts and equipment for companies such as Apple Inc., Dell, Google, Huawei, Nintendo, Xiaomi, etc., is the largest OEM company in the world by both scale and revenue."[94]

The supply chain relationship between an end user like Nintendo has with its OEM is a classic example of manufacturing efficiency that can be seen in many manufacturing areas. I remember dealing with accounts that had either their manufacturing themselves or had outsourced it by using state-of-the-art supply chain management techniques. I cannot judge whether using them is good or bad for the manufacturing world; I have written the problems they had in my previous chapter, but I believe that there could be a much more efficient way OEMs can manage their production better.

There could be smart factory design companies that have their core competency on transforming old manufacturing plants into state-of-the-art, fully automated factories that can monitor their progress and also can collect data on customer satisfaction to make revisions on their plant management to make production more effective for their next-generation products.

---

94 "Original Equipment Manufacturer." Wikipedia. Wikimedia Foundation, May 31, 2019.

If smart manufacturing can be itemized, it will bring value to companies that use it as a marketing campaign as a sign that the product they are selling is made from a state-of-the-art factory. This kind of marketing technique can be seen in Whole Foods Market, where their price for organic products are marked higher than regular products. I am not a farming expert to know whether organic products are better, but it sure makes me feel better that I am buying something that is claimed to have gone through a better agricultural process.

This can happen with smart manufacturing as well. Imagine if a company like Zara adopted a fully automated IoT manufacturing line that could not only produce new line-ups fast (not that their new lines are getting produced any slower than their rivals') but also have connected apps that ask their customers whether their new blazers or shirts or bags were satisfactory, and what kinds of things can be done for improvement.

The smart factory can directly receive customer complaints about improvement and use them to create options for operations and marketing managers at Zara that can help improve the design and save or incur less costs. This will allow customers to not only get better products faster and at an affordable price but also create a sense of involvement in the new product line they are being introduced to and enhance a sense of brand loyalty.

Of course, this kind of benefit will be mimicked by rivals and other retail and manufacturing companies, and this can be proliferated as a form of consulting or as a business that helps set up factories for companies that want the new ability to produce at an enhanced level.

Again, borrowing Professor Ferdows's words, "IoT will have a dynamic change in every industry and how manufacturing is done in the world"; however, he also stressed that there needs to be a company that is willing to go and bring it into fruition and turn ideas into solid results. I believe the first company that can achieve that will have the same effect as Apple had in 2007, which catapulted them to be the world's most valuable company in the world.[95]

SO, HOW WILL THIS IMPACT OUR FUTURE LIKE THE BOOK SAYS IN 2030?

So all in all, yes, the future is more complex. This is because we are looking at a very connected world where human activities need to be more efficient and safer. IoT will bring possibilities for companies to produce at a new level at a cheaper cost while also improving the work conditions in agriculture and manufacturing. IoT can be infused in places that have been around our lives for so long and have not experienced

---

95   "The World's Most Valuable Brands." Forbes. Forbes Magazine. Accessed June 5, 2019.

any innovation when companies that are dubbed "technology companies" are offering solutions that are innovating and disrupting the way business is done. But now with affordable sensor technology being proliferated, IoT can offer solutions where every industry will be "technology savvy" where I hope there won't be barriers to access of this technology.

Imagine a world where farmers can produce goods better, easier, and cheaper and public schools will be able to deliver foods much fresher and are able to provide children with better food on the same budget they are operating. Technology can solve problems that we are all waiting for the solutions for, and I believe that IoT can be the trigger that can disseminate it to the public. Companies like Zara already have tremendous information flowing in their operations to make sure that every new design can be created and be ready on the shelves of their international stores within weeks because they understand that the value of being flexible can trump any cost-cutting measures that can hinder any velocity they have in following the ever-changing trends in the world of fashion.

I believe the business operations that is done by efficient companies like Zara, can also be implemented on a smaller scale, and IoT will be able to help smaller businesses scale more efficiently. This technology will enable small businesses to have better understanding of using their production capacity by being more in tune with the fluctuations of the demand and also the current flow of supply through these sensor technologies. These companies can utilize their store, plant, or retail space much more effectively and be more flexible. Flexibility is always the key in making sure that you capture the demand faster than your rivals. By being flexible, you get to understand your customers better and can deal with uncertainties because you have that special ability, that adaptive capacity, to make sure you can make that transition to satisfy your customers.

However, we must also consider that increased connectivity can leave us more open to undisclosed threats as well. Farmers and manufacturers must also be aware of hacking and cyberterrorism that companies like Google and Facebook is defending against. Cyber security will be also a key area that will be growing with the booming IoT market, and I would like to stress on it in the following section.

CYBERSECURITY

Of all the topics we have spoken about in the future of the world with IoT devices, there must be issues of security in cyberspace. The fact is that data is being gathered via sponsors of IoT devices in mass-produced products on municipal and grander scales. It is not an exaggeration to be more worried about the amount of data that is being gathered that could be considered private by some individual or an entity.

We have talked about 5G, that the platform for faster networks could potentially bring a stage for content that can help transfer data in real time for virtual hospitals and MedTech devices and help autonomous driving vehicles to become a reality. However, when 5G is implemented, there must be some precautionary steps that need to be taken since this could potentially give birth to IoT devices that gather information that could be viewed as a breach of privacy. This chapter is written in the premise that 5G can be a stepping-stone for this to happen, and below will be a brief story and information I have received about 5G from a session held by a think tank in Washington, DC.

On May 21, 2019 there was an event at the Center for Strategic and International Studies (CSIS), a Washington, DC-based think tank, called "Beyond Technology: The Fourth Industrial Revolution in the Developing World"[96] that dealt with important issues of cyber security issues from IoT devices. What the event said, and what I thought was very similar, was that yes, if we have these sensor technologies integrated into our lives, it could gift humanity with better productivity.

I have mentioned earlier that the IoT will help farmers increase their crops by using sensor technology to reduce the likelihood of wasting water and resources needed for farming and can pick the crops at a much faster and precise manner. The health-care industry was also mentioned in the previous chapters as a potential benefactor from the IoT connectivity. Healthcare can be more prevalent and affordable to people because consumers can buy devices with sensors

---

96   Tuesday, May 21. "Beyond Technology: The Fourth Industrial Revolution in the Developing World." Beyond Technology: The Fourth Industrial Revolution in the Developing World | Center for Strategic and International Studies, May 15, 2019.

that enable health conditions to be monitored in advanced. These are all ways of making people smarter, more productive, and healthier.

However, what we also have to realize is the security concerns from revamping industries with technology. The IoT technology-infused economy will not only change the way people behave but also how the companies that produce these products understand the nature of the technology-infused industry. If a car company is producing a self-driving vehicle, the company is no longer making a car that can be driven by people, but a computer that drives people to destinations. If you think about making a computer that can drive people through intricate sets of connectivity with sensor technology, the security risks and concerns that are necessary will be easier to form.

From the discussions I have attended and also heard from all the professionals that I have gotten to meet over the past months of writing this book, technology moves at lightning speed. Such velocity may seem like a natural phenomenon from the private sector alone, but there must also be a sense of urgency and importance shown in how prepared the infrastructure and policies are set up for these technologies to pick up speed. Hence, engagement between the public and private sectors is critical to make sure that industry grows.

THE IMPLEMENTATION OF THE NEW NETWORK AND PRIVACY

I was at an event at CSIS called "Mitigating Security Risks to Emerging 5G Networks" on February 6, 2019.[97]

The panelists at the event were people that were highly involved in 5G and IoT businesses. From FCC Commissioner Jessica Rosenworcel to Ambassador Rob Strayer from the State Department, to Chris Boyer (AT&T), John Costello (DHS), and Travis Russell (Oracle). Security and next generation wireless networks are a key matter of discussion when it comes to 5G. US national security is to have a set of secure networks; because of the nature of the cloud system, having a secure network is pivotal.

This brings 5G interconnectivity to the highest diplomatic matter and needs to be a private and public collaboration for it to safely launch into the public. Industrial development in set to be the cornerstone of 5G, and that means a set of standards needs to be set prior to such industrial connectivity taking place. The session clearly stressed that nations must work with players that are trustworthy to make sure that 5G offers a safe way of digitizing the industrial revolution. 5G will not only bring higher connectivity but will also bring a

---

97 "Mitigating Security Risks to Emerging 5G Networks." Mitigating Security Risks to Emerging 5G Networks | Center for Strategic and International Studies. Accessed May 21, 2019.

hyper-globalization into fruition where it will impact every aspect of the ecosystems, from bio-medicine to supply chain management. 5G is still in its infancy, and there needs to be a normalized standard that so that countries that value competition can make sure that next-generation telecommunications gets introduced with fair market practices.

Business practices of different countries when implementing the new network cause problems in cybersecurity because different countries see privacy matters differently. For example, it's obvious that many countries consider data mining as a critical part of national security; there can be countries that might be more lenient on businesses collect and use data for business profits and national security but there are countries that do not view this lightly. The CSIS event I attended was centered around the current tensions between China and the US with a breach on IP issues. Like I said, China's authoritarian way of industrializing 5G, puts leniency on data mining while US does not. Such difference in views cause a hindrance in business and economic relations between the two countries. There was an example provided by Travis Russell (from Oracle) that Chinese companies like Huawei and ZTE conduct unfair practices by using the Chinese government's money to lobby developing countries to win contracts for 5G projects.

There needs to be a normalized standard set up so that countries that value competition make sure that next-generation telecommunications get introduced with fair practices. Competition should be welcomed but should be done fairly. There needs to be a coalition of states that can foster such control and set principles so that other countries can have a fair shot at industrializing their economy with 5G technology.

Arming a set of standards for privacy protection after the network launches is costly and dangerous for everyone in the world. Companies can be exposed to threats and billions of dollars of wealth can be wiped out. Hence, there needs to be a tighter control and cooperation between private and public sectors to make sure that such standards are intact before the network launches.

STATE ENTITY AND PRIVATE COMPANIES

When it comes to issue with privacy from gathering data from devices, the same companies that provide the networks for such fast transfers of data should be involved as well. For example, in the United States, players such as the FCC, the State Department, think tanks (CSIS), the Department of Homeland Security, network carriers, and technology companies should all be involved in setting standards to make sure that any potential breaches of privacy can be avoided with the right set of policies.

However, if the government is involved too deeply in implementing the policy, there could be time lags that can halt any technological disruptions from taking place. The information technology industry relies heavily on speed and timing. Just because you have the technology doesn't mean that you can make a profit by taking too much time before it comes to fruition. Although there must be a need for increased control for 5G, private companies must join the process of setting standards so that industry development can still maintain its speed of implementation before the US and other developed countries lose their competitive advantage.

Example of China's unfair practices hinder any other countries from entering the 5G projects in a fair competition. Data and information are the oil of the twenty-first century, and there are continued allegations and stories coming out from the media that China was using its authoritarian ways to gain access to information and leverage it to benefit the state's own interests. Companies like Huawei are being legally scrutinized and cast aside from key 5G projects from countries like Europe to make sure risk is mitigated from the issue of "trust" within key players in the race for 5G.

There is collaborative work going on in cybersecurity for 5G. FCC Commissioner Jessica Rosenworcel in the event mentioned that a joint venture with many government institutions (like the State Department, Department of Homeland

Security, and the FCC) and private companies (like telecommunications carriers and semiconductor and cloud companies). There is work to build security in the build-up phase.

For the first time, security is integrated into a network system before it is launched, in the standards. Standards are repeatable processes to make sure that all technology can be passed on in multiple areas. The task force should work on identifying where there is a problem in a broad supply chain risk management.

NONMARKET ENVIRONMENT AND MARKET ENVIRONMENT FOR INNOVATION AND CYBERSECURITY

Government and private collaboration are pivotal when new technology that will shape the foundation of how we connect is about to be introduced to the world. Without the government setting standards and government institutions being active in working with private companies, the very fabric of supply chain and business ecosystems will run into cascading problems that will cause detrimental ripple effects across the world. The event at CSIS and other professionals at that event gave me an extremely enlightening experience on how serious government and private collaboration is needed to ensure a safer world for growth. It is fascinating to see that respected institutions around the world are learning from the struggles faced during generations of network technologies and are trying to make sure that 5G will be done correctly.

5G is a technology that will be not be seen in the public eye but will be a more of an infrastructure for other industries like IoT to take place. This will mean that companies and societies will be existing on the cloud, on the network, and on the whole way of life for everyone. This will become the betterment for everyone if the standards are set correctly beforehand.

CYBERSECURITY MEASURES WITH TECHNOLOGY DEVELOPMENT

I was attending ITS Americas 28th Annual Meeting about "Intelligence Mobility: Safer. Greener. Smarter" held at the Walter E. Washington Convention Center in Washington, DC, from June 4–7. There I was, sitting in a session called "What Can the Transportation Industry Learn from Cyber Security of other Sectors?" It was a session formed of panels that are highly respected in the cyber security area. Since IoT will touch the development of the way people can have increased access toward mobility via autonomous vehicles, there must be a new holistic approach toward fixing a problem by only focusing on a conventional and specific vulnerability in an exploding connectivity. I would like to share what I learned from that session as below.

Pervasiveness of IoT created the need to not rely on traditional methods of cyber security. Things that bring convenience can be a threat. Things that can be so benign can be open to possibilities of threats. It's great to know that your refrigerator is telling you that its filter needs to be changed, but it also opens your connectivity toward a network that is unprotected and is growing exponentially.

There are significant advances in the alertness of the issues that are present in the IoT industry. However, how do we get a grasp on what kind of issues are present that threaten cyber security?

IoT is expanding the nature of society, and the systems are becoming more vulnerable to cyberattacks. From transportation, to banking, to retail, all sectors are now connected in ways where the network can be penetrated easier than the conventional method of security.

The thing about technology is that it disrupts the market in ways that the old method is broken for the new. The safety measures were tuned to the older sections which means the security measures are compromised since the new method of connectivity has changed how the network is connected.

We are in a world where there is a transaction happening between machines in the financial world. Therefore, educating the employees and the workforce to be more alert about cyber security measures, like being aware of emails that carry malicious software, will not be a foolproof plan to prevent any cybersecurity breaches. Simple measures such as incorporating a culture of being prepared for cybersecurity breaches can be extremely potent against any security threats.

Most of the preventative measures usually do not take a lot of complex modeling to create solutions. However, the increased connectivity will tend to make things more complicated and it's the ability to organize such intricate data to our advantage that will make the difference. For example, knowing how data mining and data analytics can be used and also know grounds in which the data we collect is vulnerable to be compromised within the open communications network. It will no longer be about avoiding malicious emails but about integrating a sense of security towards the operations (legacy supply chains for raw materials as well) that involves any connected devices. Just because you have had a long, fruitful relationship with your supplier in your supply chain, you must still revisit how security measures are done in the sense of mobility and delivery of the goods with increased use of devices for a transparent/efficient operation.

It's evident to know by now that world digital connectivity is coming on a grander scale and it is inevitable. As digital connectivity is becoming more open and prevalent, it brings challenge for cybersecurity. There needs to be better ways to detect anomalies in transactions and pattern movement to pick out any threats in cybersecurity. For example, with the IoT bringing the world to be exponentially connected, the way can do business can be open to malicious cyber-attacks. Of which, a conventional shipping company can now be hacked since there are devices that are interconnected to the vast network which is used to monitor their shipment details in real time across the world.

CHEAPER CONNECTIVITY AND CLOUD CREATE THE NEED FOR SECURITY COMPANIES

IoT is a set of devices that are interconnect to each other to provide value and convenience to the users. The primary reason for this possibility is because connectivity is getting cheaper. Companies like Cloudflare, a San Francisco-based cloud service provider, provide secure connection through the usage of sensors that are dialing into the network. Cloudflare sizes millions of requests that way and partners with IBM sensors in a serverless layer, since the higher connectivity will enable firms to exist on the web, and that allows faster computing. This will lower the cost of sensors, making more and more companies benefit from the cloud by not operating their own infrastructure.

"Cloudflare's Mutual Authentication (TLS Client Authentication) creates a secure connection between an Internet of Things device and its origin. When a device attempts to establish a connection with its origin server, Cloudflare validates the device's certificate."[98]

Successful IoT Device Authentication

IoT Device uses client certificate to authenticate itself to Cloudflare

Cloudflare only allows devices with certificates signed by device manufacturers root CA

If the device has a valid client certificate, like having the correct key to enter a building, the device is able to establish a secure connection.

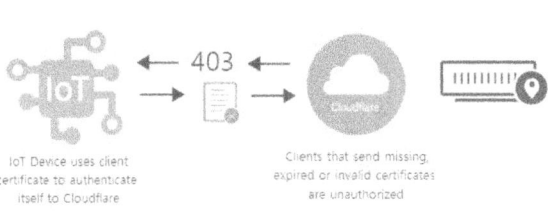

Unsuccessful IoT Device Authentication

403

IoT Device uses client certificate to authenticate itself to Cloudflare

Clients that send missing, expired or invalid certificates are unauthorized

---

98 "Orbit for Internet of Things Devices." Cloudflare. Accessed May 21, 2019.

If the device's certificate is missing, expired, or invalid, the connection is revoked and Cloudflare returns a 403 error.[99]

Not only does Cloudflare work as a bouncer between you and the people that are using your information, but it also protects and accelerates any website online. Since 5G will enable companies to exist online, the need for security is more inevitable, and if companies like Cloudflare can offer a solution to keep your site clean, fast, and protected, the digital connectivity cost will be decreased immensely for not just large MNC (multinational corporations) but also for startups to exist online and operate. Below is the excerpt from Cloudflare's website the explains what they do that makes them effective.

"Cloudflare is designed to accelerate and secure any website. Our system works somewhat like a Content Delivery Network (CDN) but is designed to be much easier to setup and configure. To explain how the system works, imagine you have a website (allen.com) and it's running a web server with the IP address of 198.51.100.1. Before Cloudflare, if someone typed your website's domain (allen.com) into their browser, the first thing that visitor's computer would do is send a query to the DNS system and get back your web server's IP address (198.51.100.1).

---

99 "Orbit for Internet of Things Devices." Cloudflare. Accessed May 21, 2019.

In order to make Cloudflare easy to set up, we take advantage of how this basic function of the Internet works. Rather than having you add hardware, install software, or change your code, we have you designate two Cloudflare nameservers as the authoritative nameservers for your domain (e.g., bob.ns.cloudflare.com and sara.ns.cloudflare.com). You make this change with the registrar from which you bought your domain (e.g., GoDaddy, Network Solutions, Register.com, etc.).

Designating Cloudflare as your authoritative nameservers doesn't change anything about your website. Your registrar remains your registrar, your hosting provider remains your hosting provider, and so on. However, because we are your authoritative nameserver, we can begin cleaning and accelerating your web traffic.

By storing your website on local data centers and blocking malicious visitors, Cloudflare can reduce your bandwidth usage by over 60 percent and reduce the number of requests to your website by 65 percent. By serving content from a data center close to the visitor and performing some extra web content optimization in that data center, we can cut in half the average page load time."[100]

---

100 "How Does Cloudflare Work?" Cloudflare Support. Accessed May 21, 2019.

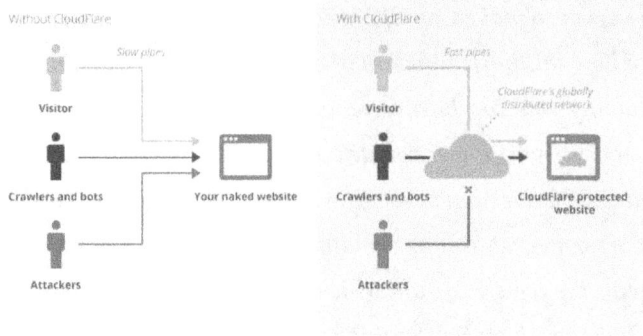

All in all, I was very fortunate to be in the MBA program at Georgetown, as I was able to visit and learn about the dynamics of the IoT industry and the companies that are offering security solutions like Cloudflare. Also, I was able to attend many of the sessions held by various think tanks in Washington, DC, that deal with security issues with 5G and IoT. Culminating on all of my experiences and combining them with the discussions I had with many professionals working at IT companies (former consultants and employees that were working on projects with these tech companies), I believe security risks should be a factor that cannot be taken lightly.

If you think about it in the simplest context, IoT is basically using plethora of data about your behavior through sensors, in multiple devices that you are wearing or using daily, to discern or recommend a course of action or a set of purchasing options in the future. Some can call this a breach of privacy given that your behavior is constantly being monitored or being sold for commercial purposes. Although IoT will be used on a grand scale (to manage traffic in public sectors to effectively develop infrastructures, there are underlying concerns about how the data is being used and treated when people are giving away information about their daily lives.

I once attended a session at Brookings Institute in Washington, DC, about "How China and the US Are Advancing Artificial Intelligence" on March 12, 2019.[101] The panels consisted of people from Brookings Institute and Intel Corporation and was about how artificial intelligence algorithms are using the data collected from sensors and cameras around China and the US. Robb Gordon, who was on one of the panels and is the senior policy director and legal counsel at Intel Corporation said that (and I am summarizing because I took down notes) technology from implementation of devices and AI is changing people's lives in China; cities in China are surrounded by multiple cameras that gather data and have AI to create efficient ways of traveling and also provide services like security and record payments to be saved for future conveniences. Although much discussion was on the basis of the potential the IoT devices will bring when coupled with AI, the panels all agreed that there needs to be action

---

101 "How China and the U.S. Are Advancing Artificial Intelligence." Brookings. Brookings, March 14, 2019.

to protect people's privacy but at the same time have the AI be effectively in use for the public.

I agree with the fact that there needs to be a sense of privacy protection, and many companies like Cloudflare or government entities like the FCC are trying to make sure that sufficient standards are made so that the new era of connectivity will bring a sense of security toward using people's data. However, we also have to cautious that this technology will bring wealth and convenience to key aspects of life like health care, finance, education, national security, and traveling; hence, we have to make sure technology standards are met to prevent any information spillage for exploitation but at the same time make sure that it does not hinder or bar the advancement of society.

SO, HOW WILL THIS IMPACT OUR FUTURE LIKE THE BOOK SAYS IN 2030?

The world is going to become more connected. IoT, 5G, digital transformation of the society we know will be inevitable, and we need to put as much effort into knowing the risks involved as much as we would like to discuss the abundant benefits that this future will bring to our lives.

The risks that are involved can be catastrophic or minimal depending on how well-informed the public is. So in the future, like the book says in 2030, I do hope that authors like me can inform the public enough of the current work that is being done to make sure that the future operating in a grandiose connectivity will be safe and will not end up giving up more than it gains from these implementations. When the IoT becomes prevalent, every business professional across all industries will have to know that cybersecurity in their part will no longer be about avoiding malicious emails or having malware detection software to be installed in every computer in their company.

The future of security in a hyperconnected world of IoT is about integrating a sense of security toward the operations (legacy supply chains for raw materials as well) that involves any connected devices. Just because you have had a long, fruitful relationship with your supplier in your supply chain, you must still revisit how security measures are done in the sense of mobility and delivery of the goods with increased used of devices for a transparent/efficient operation.

This means that the world will more be sensitive toward how we view trust with people not only in business supply chains but also with customers in day to day transactions. Trust will be more than just a mere transaction with the world of IoT and connectivity; it's about becoming a whole together, with entire operations of business working in unison where all matters of operations (not just products) become interoperable. Businesses should always consider the safety of not just their own but also the safety of those that they do their business with.

CONCLUSION

———

I have tried my best to articulate what changes will happen with the new technology and how it will most likely change the way we live our lives. If you go to the technology section in any of the news outlets, I assure you that there will always be new developing stories about either 5G or artificial intelligence. These sectors are growing fast and are making strides in their development influencing how business leaders today are making decisions.

How these existing technologies are being incorporated is also very important, and I believe this is where most people fail to see the potential of IoT. I am a student of business who loves being trained in the art of selling technology and looking for new insights in finding the "next big thing" on the market, and through my course of career it is not an exaggeration to say that we will be living in a more connected world than we ever imagined to be.

YOUR HOME

IoT will be the industry that will bring the futuristic lifestyle to everyone. Just imagine having your all of your devices and home appliances communicating with one another to move more cohesively to understand your (the customer's) needs better. A tailored life, a life when you wake up and your devices will automatically have the shower ready and your toaster will be making you breakfast and have your calendar set up on the refrigerator screen for you to see what needs to done today.

You will no longer have to face the hassle of making minuscule decisions and can move on to what's important and make priorities so that you can be productive beyond your imagination. It's a future where you have your own Jarvis just like Iron Man!

The concept of a tailored life can happen in many different ways. I have focused on smart homes, smart cities, and Med-Tech fields as an example of where the possibilities are most viable and impactful in our daily lives.

I have talked about smart homes where your appliances will be able to communicate with each other to provide a home that is completely automated to suit the needs of every person who is working. No one has to walk into a dark and cold (or hot and humid) apartment after work; they can now choose to have the apartment lit up before they enter it and have the kitchen be ready to cook the moment, they open the door.

Same goes for the streets as well. There has to be a better way of handling traffic; anyone who has been stuck in rush hour traffic should know how bad it is. Having multiple sensors embedded in cities will enable real-time knowledge of where the traffic congestion is by gathering thousands of real time data on traffic and recommending options to alleviate the traffic by diverting it away to different routes. Similarly, IoT can be used to control traffic lights to make sure that traffic is freed up sooner.

This level of convenience can also work with your medicine as well. IoT will enable you to have a virtual meeting with your doctor for routine checkups from your home since there will be wearable devices that can take the place of medical devices that are used in hospitals for simple checkups. Also, as I stated earlier in the book, by incorporating sensors in every medicine that is being manufactured, there can be enough knowledge of what kind of medication is being prescribed and where the cheapest and closest pharmacy is whenever you feel sick.

YOUR WORK

Businesses (especially small to mid-sized ones) can also adopt this technology to improve their operations by using these sensor technologies to monitor their business processes in real time to ensure speed, precision, and flexibility in delivering the goods that the customer wants.

Being able to justify the use of technology to bring value to the customers is why I love studying business and the IoT industry: it can bring better value to our society. For example, I am hearing stories that local farmers in Asia that have adopted IoT technology to track their crops through their smartphones and can program their sprinklers to increase the amount of water sprayed on their crops while away from their farm. Also, these local farmers don't have to be on their farm all day during the blazing heat because sensors implanted across their crops can tell the farmer how much the crops are growing and can alert them if there are any anomalies. This can save tremendous amounts of time for the farmer and can liberate individual entrepreneurs to have more time to work on other aspects and to save resources on petty things for their day-to-day tasks.

IoT can also improve supply chain management across different suppliers and businesses around the world. When I was speaking with founders of start-up companies near the DC area, I was amazed by how many small companies were involved in various supply chains. Whether you are a coffee roaster company that is serving nitro cold-brew coffee, or you provide mapping services online, all companies were a part of a much bigger business chain that links each on a grander scale.

When it comes to supply chains in a multinational corporation, it will be easier to track goods that are being shipped from one supplier to the next; however, small companies do not have such resources at their disposal to track every detail of their product from raw materials to finished products throughout their supply chain. But if the products and manufacturing phases at each phase of the supply chain were equipped with sensors to track and monitor its process in real time and share its progress to all the players in the supply chain, big and small players in the market will have the same resources to track and nimbly update their processes to ensure that customers can get their products the way they wanted, fast. In this, IoT can open up multiple possibilities to make the business world run much smoother.

I hope by the time this book gets out, 5G has rolled out enough where people start looking into new platforms and contents that can be shared with others through this massive connectivity. I also hope people will be driving safer cars and cars that themselves are more self-aware of the dangers that their drivers can face and can make smart recommendations. I also hope people will be more knowledgeable of the benefits that can come from devices becoming more synced with their preferences and be more excited to find out what incumbent devices and appliances can be improved with sensor technology to give a much more tailored life for the individuals.

However, what I really hope is that people are not too skeptical about sharing their data to service providers in the IoT industry. Today, in the news, there are a lot of alarming stories dealing with breaches in people's data and privacy matters. I am not going to name companies or entities that are responsible for these atrocious acts, but I do know that there will be more of these incidents if we as a society collectively fail to acknowledge the potential of data gathering and work to secure our previous lives for the betterment of the future.

The concept of the IoT industry is basically sensor technology. It is inevitable that you have to provide your life routine and your personal preferences that amounts to abundant data that is extremely valuable. And it is scary whenever you hear stories in the news that companies have misused data that is being provided by its users for all sorts of malicious activities.

Cybersecurity is an area that needs a lot of attention and improvement if IoT is to go global, and I do not doubt that there will be services for this area that will protect data without having to worry about someone stealing someone's precious data.

Like I have said in my earlier chapters, data is becoming more valuable throughout the day, and I have been taught at Georgetown University that data's value has surpassed oil. Putting this valuable data to good use is very important if the world would like to see profit from this asset.

I believe IoT can bring this to fruition. I believe it's the way of the future, and with the right set of policy and business minds, it will shape the world in ways that will enhance the human ability beyond what we have seen throughout the decade and unleash the next industrial revolution that we have waited for so long.

If this world hasn't come by the time you've read this book, then you are lucky! Join the movement!

ACKNOWLEDGMENTS

———

First and foremost, I would like to thank my wife for her unconditional love and support. Without her, I would have never pursued my passion for the technology industry.

Creating this book was one of the greatest journeys that I have ever embarked on. I have had the unique and very fulfilling opportunity to meet and study the new and rising industry in technology before it becomes visible in our everyday lives. Each people I have spoken with gave me tremendous learning experience, and I would like to acknowledge Professor Kasra Ferdows, Professor especially Mark Giordano, Professor Jung Gil Ko, Ben Edwards, Chris Magnan, and all the people who I work with at Samsung for sharing their knowledge. For all those who I have spoken to, please know that I have not forgotten you, and you have my utmost respect and gratitude.

I want to thank my family for always supporting me, and for believing that I can accomplish whatever I set my mind on. I often overextend myself, but my family has always been there to help me stay calm and trust the process throughout this journey. I want to thank my friends who have supported me throughout this journey and have helped share my book and get the word out.

I want to thank my editors, Linda Berardelli, Leila Summers, and Grzegorz Laszczyk for continuing to work with me even though I can be extremely stressful at times with last-minute changes. I would also like to thank Professor Eric Koester and Brian Bies for their leadership and guiding me whenever I had problems with my book.

Lastly, I want to acknowledge my MBA classmates at Georgetown University (class of 2020) and anyone who has pre-ordered this book, I have received so much support from all of you that I simply don't have enough space to write all my gratitude; but do know that I will be personally thanking you once this book is released. This book is the first step for me into a brighter future in this industry. I am currently working on other projects that I hope people continue to follow.

Thank you,
Chong Hwan Kim

CITATIONS

———

IOT AND WHY?

"Industrial Revolution." Wikipedia. Wikimedia Foundation, April 30, 2019. https://en.wikipedia.org/wiki/Industrial_Revolution.

Fitch, Asa. "Nvidia to Acquire Mellanox, Its Biggest Deal Ever at Roughly $7 Billion." The Wall Street Journal. Dow Jones & Company, March 11, 2019. https://www.wsj.com/articles/nvidia-to-acquire-mellanox-for-about-7-billion-11552304615?fbclid=IwAR0T2vE-Bwf2kr4XGIqiEpiTblE5p-TVFZ8TJx6l_dinBxnLc5FJ-fUTF72mk.

"Mellanox Technologies." Wikipedia. Wikimedia Foundation, October 5, 2019. https://en.wikipedia.org/wiki/Mellanox_Technologies.

"Cloud Computing." Wikipedia. Wikimedia Foundation, October 22, 2019. https://en.wikipedia.org/wiki/Cloud_computing.

"5G." Wikipedia. Wikimedia Foundation, October 25, 2019. https://en.wikipedia.org/wiki/5G.

"Verizon 5G: This Is 5G Built Right." Verizon. Accessed October 27, 2019. https://www.verizonwireless.com/5g/?cmp=KNC-C-HQ-NON-R-AC-NONE-NONE-2K0PX0-PX-GAW-71700000048123830&ds_rl=1264246&gclid=CjoKCQjw_r3nBRDxARIsAJljle-HlAsN6I-wRrUesJn4VLiS--6-VqKgIBGvDVejsmdLvQ_ENuqRkofoaAs2tEALw_wcB&gclsrc=aw.ds.

Lcrenshaw. "2016 Sustainability Forum." U.S. Chamber of Commerce Foundation, October 24, 2019. https://www.uschamberfoundation.org/event/2016-sustainability-forum.

"Climate Change and Population Growth Are Making the World's Water Woes More Urgent." The Economist. The Economist Newspaper, February 28, 2019. https://

www.economist.com/special-report/2019/02/28/climate-change-and-population-growth-are-making-the-worlds-water-woes-more-urgent.

Cooper, and Brent. "The Abstraction of Water." Medium. The Abs-Tract Organization, February 18, 2018. https://medium.com/the-abs-tract-organization/the-abstraction-of-water-68510e720985.

Fishman, Charles. "Water Is Broken. Data Can Fix It." The New York Times. March 17, 2016. https://www.nytimes.com/2016/03/17/opinion/the-water-data-drought.html.

"Water Facts." Save The Water™. Accessed May 19, 2019. http://savethewater.org/education-resources/water-facts/.

"Efficient Irrigation | Water Saving Irrigation Methods." Water Use It Wisely. Accessed May 19, 2019. https://wateruseitwisely.com/100-ways-to-conserve/landscape-care/principles-of-xeriscape-design/efficient-irrigation/.

"World Development Report 2009." WDRs - World Development Report 2009. Accessed May 19, 2019. http://web.worldbank.org/WBSITE/EXTERNAL/EXTDEC/EXTRESEARCH/EXTWDRS/0,,-

contentMDK:23062295~pagePK:478093~piP-
K:477627~theSitePK:477624,00.html.

"What Is a Smart City and How Can a City Boost Its IQ?"
World Bank Blogs. Accessed May 19, 2019. http://blogs.
worldbank.org/sustainablecities/what-is-a-smart-city-
and-how-can-a-city-boost-its-iq.

"About US." ABI Research: for visionaries. Accessed May
19, 2019. https://www.abiresearch.com/pages/about-abi-
research/

"Smart Cities Could Lead to Cost Savings of $5 Trillion."
Information Age, May 15, 2018. https://www.informa-
tion-age.com/smart-cities-lead-cost-savings-5-tril-
lion-123469863/.

"Discover the Smart Airport That's Teaching Lessons to
Smart Cities (and See It in Action)." Smart Cities Council Accessed May 19, 2019. https://na.smartcitiescouncil.
com/article/discover-smart-airport-thats-teaching-les-
sons-smart-cities-and-see-it-action.

"Strategy for American Leadership in Advanced Manufac-
turing." Strategy for American Leadership in Advanced
Manufacturing. SUBCOMMITTEE ON ADVANCED
MANUFACTURING COMMITTEE ON TECH-

NOLOGY, October 2018. https://www.whitehouse.gov/
wp-content/uploads/2018/10/Advanced-Manufactur-
ing-Strategic-Plan-2018.pdf.

"Greek Proverb Quote 'A Society Grows Great When Old
Men Plant Trees Whose Shade They Know They Shall
Never Sit in." Wisdom Home Decor Print Wall Art."
Amazon. Amazon. Accessed May 19, 2019. https://www.
amazon.com/Greek-Proverb-Quote-society-Wisdom/
dp/B01MZX8U46.

Garfeld, Dean C, Marjorie Dickman, John Godfrey,
and Vince Jesaits. "National IOT Strategy Dialogue."
National IOT Strategy Dialogue, 2016.

"Moore's Law." Wikipedia. Wikimedia Foundation, July 22,
2019. https://en.wikipedia.org/wiki/Moore%27s_law.

"5G." Wikipedia. Wikimedia Foundation, May 19, 2019.
https://en.wikipedia.org/wiki/5G.

"Azure IoT." Microsoft Azure. Accessed May 19, 2019.
https://azure.microsoft.com/en-us/overview/iot/.

Crenshaw, Liza. "2016 Sustainability Forum." U.S. Chamber of Commerce Foundation, May 19, 2016. https://

www.uschamberfoundation.org/event/2016-sustain-ability-forum.

"Model S | Tesla." Tesla Motors. Accessed May 19, 2019. https://www.tesla.com/models.

"Water Conservation Campaign." Water Use It Wisely. Accessed May 19, 2019. https://wateruseitwisely.com/.

Zomorodi, Behsad. "How Do Clinical Wearables Impact Patient Care and Quality of Life?" Healthcare IT News, June 16, 2018. https://hitconsultant.net/2018/04/09/clini-cal-wearables-revolutionizing-care/.

5G Revolution Begins at Verizon Wireless. Accessed May 30, 2019. https://www.verizonwireless.com/5g/?cmp=KNC-C-HQ-NON-R-AC-NONE-NONE-2K0PX0-PX-GAW-71700000048123830&ds_rl=1264246&gclid=CjoKCQjw_r3nBRDxARIsAJljle-HlAsN6I-wRrUesJn4VLiS—6-VqKgIBGvDVejsmdLvQ_ENuqRkofoaAs2tEALw_wcB&gclsrc=aw.ds.

Angel, Maytaal. "Worldsteel Raises Forecast for 2018 Global Steel Demand Growth to..." Reuters. Thomson Reuters, April 17, 2018. https://www.reuters.com/article/us-global-steel-demand/worldsteel-raises-forecast-for-2018-global-steel-demand-growth-to-1-8-percent-idUSKBN1HO1DY.

CITATIONS- AT HOME

"IoT for Connected Homes | Home Automation, Home Security & Monitoring, Home Networking | AWS IoT." Amazon. Amazon. Accessed May 9, 2019. https://aws.amazon.com/ko/iot/solutions/connected-home/.

Jhonsa, Eric. "Jeff Bezos: Amazon's Market Size Is Effectively Unlimited." TheStreet, September 5, 2018. https://www.thestreet.com/opinion/5-interesting-things-shared-by-jeff-bezos-in-his-latest-interview-14703194.

"Refrigerator." Wikipedia. Wikimedia Foundation, May 5, 2019. https://en.wikipedia.org/wiki/Refrigerator.

"Smart Appliances - Worldwide | Statista Market Forecast." Statista. Accessed May 9, 2019. https://www.statista.com/outlook/389/100/smart-appliances/worldwide.

"Consumer Electronics Show." Wikipedia. Wikimedia Foundation, April 16, 2019. https://en.wikipedia.org/wiki/Consumer_Electronics_Show.

"Amazon Alexa." Wikipedia. Wikimedia Foundation, May 9, 2019. https://en.wikipedia.org/wiki/Amazon_Alexa.

Dalton, Matthew. "Is Time Running Out for the Swiss Watch Industry?" The Wall Street Journal. Dow Jones & Company, March 12, 2018. https://www.wsj.com/articles/is-time-running-out-for-the-swiss-watch-industry-1520867714.

"Distracted Driving and Transportation Security." Distracted Driving and Transportation Security | MC Tank Transport, Inc. Accessed May 9, 2019. https://www.mctank.com/blog.php?27.

IronsExpert. "Smart Kitchens a Reality - IOT." Medium. Medium, February 25, 2018. https://medium.com/@ironsexpert/smart-kitchen-reality-internet-of-things-ee914bde8ad6.

Farrell, Maureen. "SoftBank, Other Investors in Talks to Invest $1 Billion in Uber's Self-Driving Unit." The Wall Street Journal. Dow Jones & Company, March 13, 2019. https://www.wsj.com/articles/softbank-other-investors-in-talks-to-invest-1-billion-in-ubers-self-driving-unit-11552515631?mod=hp_lead_pos5.

Carter, Jamie. "CES 2019: All the Latest News and Reviews." TechRadar. TechRadar, January 11, 2019. https://www. techradar.com/news/ces-2019.

Kanellos, Michael. "Hold The Laughter: Why The Smart Fridge Is A Great Idea." Forbes. Forbes Magazine, January 13, 2016. https://www.forbes.com/sites/michael-kanellos/2016/01/13/hold-the-laughter-why-the-smart-fridge-is-a-great-idea/#3a9051a17d40.

Midrack, Renée Lynn. "What Is so Smart About a Smart Fridge?" Lifewire. Lifewire, April 30, 2019. https://www. lifewire.com/smart-refrigerator-4158327.

Sawicki, Donald S. Braking Factors. Accessed May 9, 2019. https://copradar.com/redlight/factors/.

"Smart Appliances - Worldwide | Statista Market Forecast." Statista. Accessed May 9, 2019. https://www. statista.com/outlook/389/100/smart-appliances/world-wide#market-users.

"Smart Appliances - Worldwide | Statista Market Forecast." Statista. Accessed May 9, 2019. https://www.statista. com/outlook/389/100/smart-appliances/worldwide.

Dalton, Matthew. "Is Time Running Out for the Swiss Watch Industry?" The Wall Street Journal. Dow Jones & Company, March 12, 2018. https://www.wsj.com/articles/is-time-running-out-for-the-swiss-watch-industry-1520867714.

Pdcteam. "Reaction Time." PoliceDriver.Com, October 29, 2016. https://policedriver.com/reaction-time/.

Thursday, May 16. "America's Global Infrastructure Opportunity: Three Recommendations to the New U.S. Development Finance Corporation." America's Global Infrastructure Opportunity: Three Recommendations to the New U.S. Development Finance Corporation | Center for Strategic and International Studies, October 12, 2018. https://www.csis.org/events/americas-global-infrastructure-opportunity-three-recommendations-new-us-development-finance.

"Global Medtech R&D Spending Medtech Revenue Share 2011-2024 | Statistic." Statista. Accessed May 23, 2019. https://www.statista.com/statistics/309305/worldwide-medtech-research-and-development-spending-as-percent-of-revenue/.

Brown, Ian, and Andrew A Adams. "The Ethical Challenges of Ubiquitous Healthcare." International review of information Ethics, December 2017.

Zomorodi, Behsad. "How Do Clinical Wearables Impact Patient Care and Quality of Life?" Healthcare IT News, June 16, 2018. https://hitconsultant.net/2018/04/09/clinical-wearables-revolutionizing-care/.

Pennic, Fred. "Philips to Acquire Carestream Health's Health IT Business Unit." Healthcare IT News, March 11, 2019. https://hitconsultant.net/2019/03/07/philips-acquires-carestream-hcis-business/#.XIcDeihKjic.

"The Bleeding Edge." Wikipedia. Wikimedia Foundation, April 19, 2019. https://en.wikipedia.org/wiki/The_Bleeding_Edge.

"The Bleeding Edge." Netflix Official Site, July 27, 2018. https://www.netflix.com/watch/80170862?trackId=13752289&tctx=0%2C0%2C7453fb2faaba7f1f577e9bd30b15fb5a649f8cf1%3A54521ab2f9d6033645df58fbf90000a7416b53ed%2C%2C.

"Our Technology." Fitbit. Accessed May 23, 2019. https://www.fitbit.com/technology.

Zogbi, Dennis M. "The Global Market for Medical Electronics and Outlook to 2022."TTI, February 28, 2017. https://www.ttiinc.com/content/ttiinc/en/resources/marketeye/categories/passives/me-zogbi-20170228.html.

CITATIONS- AT WORK

Agrawal, Ajay, Joshua Gans, and Avi Goldfarb. *Prediction Machines: the Simple Economics of Artificial Intelligence.* Boston, MA: Harvard Business Review Press, 2018.

"Automating Intelligently Is Tesla's Manufacturing Advantage." CleanTechnica, June 26, 2018. https://cleantechnica.com/2018/06/30/automating-intelligently-is-teslas-manufacturing-advantage/.

Academy, IBM Think. "How It Works: The Internet of Things and Manufacturing." YouTube. YouTube, November 10, 2016. https://www.youtube.com/watch?v=R5RfSQ3Nxzg.

Anixter. "What Is Industry 4.0 and Smart Manufacturing?" YouTube. YouTube, May 9, 2018. https://www.youtube.com/watch?v=EV1Ygw6_rCs.

Whang, Seungjin, Hide Saito, Steve Van Horne, Casey Koshijima, and Takafumi Ueda. "SEVEN-ELEVEN

JAPAN." Stanford: STANFORD GRADUATE
SCHOOL OF BUSINESS, May 23, 2006.

Tech in Asia - Connecting Asia's startup ecosystem.
Accessed October 28, 2019. https://www.techinasia.com/
startup-failure-analysis.

Yoohooo. "세상 모든 새로움의 시작, KT 5G 스마트 팩토리."
늘 곁에 kt, KT그룹 블로그. TISTORY, February 12, 2019.
https://blog.kt.com/1282.

Staff, Motley Fool. "What Is Algorithmic Trading?" The
Motley Fool. The Motley Fool, April 27, 2017. https://
www.fool.com/knowledge-center/what-is-algorith-
mic-trading.aspx.

"STRATEGY FOR AMERICAN LEADERSHIP IN
ADVANCED MANUFACTURING." *STRATEGY FOR
AMERICAN LEADERSHIP IN ADVANCED MANU-
FACTURING*, SUBCOMMITTEE ON ADVANCED
MANUFACTURING COMMITTEE ON TECHNOL-
OGY, Oct. 2018, www.whitehouse.gov/wp-content/
uploads/2018/10/Advanced-Manufacturing-Strate-
gic-Plan-2018.pdf.

"Organic Food Sales in the U.S. 2017 | Statista." Statista. Accessed May 30, 2019. https://www.statista.com/statistics/196952/organic-food-sales-in-the-us-since-2000/.

Tesla. "Model Y Unveil." YouTube. YouTube, March 15, 2019. https://www.youtube.com/watch?v=Tb_Wn6KouVs.

Gongloff, Mark. "ISMs Svengali-Like Hold on the Stock Market." The Wall Street Journal. Dow Jones & Company, May 31, 2011. https://blogs.wsj.com/marketbeat/2011/05/31/isms-svengali-like-hold-on-the-stock-market/.

"The Advanced Manufacturing National Program Office." Manufacturing.gov. Accessed May 30, 2019. https://www.manufacturing.gov/partners/advanced-manufacturing-national-program-office.

Getty. "Amazon Is Working on a Pair of Google Glass-Style Smart Glasses Powered by Alexa." mirror, September 20, 2017. https://www.mirror.co.uk/tech/amazon-working-pair-google-glass-11207169.

Mythemes. "Jeff Bezos | Stephenson Blogs on Internet of Things - Internet of Things Strategy, Breakthroughs and Management." Stephenson blogs on Internet of

Things. Accessed May 30, 2019. http://www.stephenson-strategies.com/tag/jeff-bezos/.

"Microsoft's Satya Nadella Reckons the World's a Computer Thanks to AI and IoT Tech | TheINQUIRER." http://www.theinquirer.net, May 23, 2018. https://www.theinquirer.net/inquirer/news/3032930/microsofts-satya-nadella-reckons-the-worlds-a-computer-thanks-to-ai-and-iot-tech .

Tuesday, May 21. "Beyond Technology: The Fourth Industrial Revolution in the Developing World." Beyond Technology: The Fourth Industrial Revolution in the Developing World | Center for Strategic and International Studies, May 15, 2019. https://www.csis.org/events/beyond-technology-fourth-industrial-revolution-developing-world.

"Mitigating Security Risks to Emerging 5G Networks." Mitigating Security Risks to Emerging 5G Networks | Center for Strategic and International Studies. Accessed May 21, 2019. https://www.csis.org/analysis/mitigating-security-risks-emerging-5g-networks.

"Orbit for Internet of Things Devices." Cloudflare. Accessed May 21, 2019. https://www.cloudflare.com/orbit/.

"How Does Cloudflare Work?" Cloudflare Support. Accessed May 21, 2019. https://support.cloudflare.com/hc/en-us/articles/205177068-Step-1-How-does-Cloudflare-work-.

"How China and the U.S. Are Advancing Artificial Intelligence." Brookings. Brookings, March 14, 2019. https://www.brookings.edu/events/how-china-and-the-u-s-are-advancing-artificial-intelligence/.

Tech in Asia - Connecting Asia's startup ecosystem. Accessed November 3, 2019. http://www.techinasia.com/startup-failure-analysis.

Hansen, Suzy. "How Zara Grew Into the World's Largest Fashion Retailer." *The New York Times*, The New York Times, 9 Nov. 2012, www.nytimes.com/2012/11/11/magazine/how-zara-grew-into-the-worlds-largest-fashion-retailer.html.

Mhugos. "Zara Clothing Company Supply Chain." *SCM Globe*, 11 Mar. 2019, www.scmglobe.com/zara-clothing-company-supply-chain/.

Ferdows, Kasra, Jose A.D. Machuca, and Michael A. Lewis. "Zara: The World's Largest Fashion Retailer." Wellesley: Case Centre, 2014.

Narang, Nitant, and Procurify. "How Zara Quietly Disrupted Fashion." Spend Culture, February 21, 2018. https://blog.procurify.com/2016/10/24/supply-chain-beats-zara-spend-culture/.

"10 Trends in Digital Manufacturing Revealed in Latest Industrial IoT Survey Jointly Conducted by SME and Plataine." ManufacturingTomorrow. Accessed June 5, 2019. https://www.manufacturingtomorrow.com/story/2018/07/10-trends-in-digital-manufacturing-revealed-in-latest-industrial-iot-survey-jointly-conducted-by-sme-and-plataine/11805/.

Larsen, Marcus Moller, Toben Pedersen, and Dmitrij Slepniov. "LEGO GROUP: AN OUTSOURCING JOURNEY." Ontario: Ivey Publishing, 2010.

Coren, Michael J. "Watch Tesla Build a Giant Tent for Its New Model 3 Assembly Line in Three Weeks." Quartz. Quartz, July 10, 2018. https://qz.com/1309773/watch-tesla-build-a-massive-tent-for-its-model-3-assembly-line-in-three-weeks/.

"Tesla Factory." Wikipedia. Wikimedia Foundation, May 21, 2019. https://en.wikipedia.org/wiki/Tesla_Factory#Tesla_Model_S_manufacturing_process.

Rosoff, Matt. "Every Type of Tech Product Has Gotten Cheaper over the Last Two Decades - except for One." Business Insider. Business Insider, October 14, 2015. https://www.businessinsider.com/historical-price-trends-for-tech-products-2015-10.

"SAMSUNG POWERbot™ ROBOT VACUUM." Samsung POWERbot™ Robot Vacuum | Special Offer, Features & Specs. Accessed June 5, 2019. http://samsungpowerbot.com/?gclid=CjoKCQiAtvPjBRDPARIsAJfZzoo_b_YK1XT1mKl8zVoRgiACN78y5_Lli9vdew4t9LCOBEX-EZpXK92UaAo6cEALw_wcB&gclsrc=aw.ds.

"Azure IoT." Microsoft Azure. Accessed June 5, 2019. https://azure.microsoft.com/en-us/overview/iot/?&OCID=AID739522_SEM_jlLEYfT6_.

"Azure IoT." Microsoft Azure. Accessed June 5, 2019. https://azure.microsoft.com/en-us/overview/iot/industry/.

"iPhone." Wikipedia. Wikimedia Foundation, May 8, 2019. https://en.wikipedia.org/wiki/IPhone.

Wright, Mic. "The Original iPhone Announcement Annotated: Steve Jobs' Genius Meets Genius." The Next Web, June 12, 2018. https://thenextweb.com/apple/2015/09/09/genius-annotated-with-genius/.

"Original Equipment Manufacturer." Wikipedia. Wikimedia Foundation, May 31, 2019. https://en.wikipedia.org/wiki/Original_equipment_manufacturer.

"The World's Most Valuable Brands." Forbes. Forbes Magazine. Accessed June 5, 2019. https://www.forbes.com/powerful-brands/list/.

케이티 KT -. "KT 5G x 현대중공업 Digital Transformation." YouTube. YouTube, March 7, 2019. https://www.youtube.com/watch?v=0M1kloI3s4k.

Ries, Eric. *Lean Startup*. Place of publication not identified: Portfolio Penguin, 2017.

Rosoff, Matt. "Every Type of Tech Product Has Gotten Cheaper over the Last Two Decades - except for One." Business Insider. Business Insider, October 14, 2015. https://www.businessinsider.com/historical-price-trends-for-tech-products-2015-10.

www.ingramcontent.com/pod-product-compliance
Lightning Source LLC
Chambersburg PA
CBHW071521180526
45171CB00002B/333